BFI TV Classics

BFI TV Classics is a series of books celebrating key individual television programmes and series. Television scholars, critics and novelists provide critical readings underpinned with careful research, alongside a personal response to the programme and a case for its 'classic' status.

D1424826

CSI:
Crime Scene
Investigation

Steven
Cohan

palgrave
macmillan

A BFI book published by Palgrave Macmillan

For Linda

None of the content of this publication is intended to imply that it is endorsed by the programme's broadcaster or production companies involved.

First published in 2008 by
PALGRAVE MACMILLAN
Houndmills, Basingstoke, Hampshire RG21 6XS and
175 Fifth Avenue, New York, N.Y. 10010
Companies and Representatives throughout the world

on behalf of the

BRITISH FILM INSTITUTE
21 Stephen Street, London W1T 1LN
www.bfi.org.uk

There's more to discover about film and television through the BFI.
Our world-renowned archive, cinemas, festivals, films, publications and learning resources are here to inspire you.

PALGRAVE MACMILLAN is the global academic imprint of the Palgrave Macmillan division of St Martin's Press, LLC and of Palgrave Macmillan Ltd. Macmillan® is a registered trademark in the United States, United Kingdom and other countries.
Palgrave is a registered trademark in the European Union and other countries.

Images from *CSI*, Alliance Atlantis/CBS Paramount Network Television/CBS Productions/Jerry Bruckheimer Television/Touchstone Television.

Set by Cambrian Typesetters, Camberley, Surrey
Printed in China

This book is printed on paper suitable for recycling and made from fully managed and sustained forest sources. Logging, pulping and manufacturing processes are expected to conform to the environmental regulations of the country of origin.

British Library Cataloguing-in-Publication Data
A catalogue record for this book is available from the British Library

ISBN 978-1-84457-255-7

Contents

Introduction

The US debut of *CSI: Crime Scene Investigation* on Friday, 6 October 2000, turned out to be more promising for CBS than the network expected. Before the new season began, CBS was banking on several high-profile new shows to boost its ratings. A revival of *The Fugitive* and a Bette Midler sitcom were touted in particular, although as it turned out neither show would return for a second season. *CSI*, on the other hand, the last of the new pilots chosen by CBS, was, as *Daily Variety* noted, considered 'more iffy'.[1]

Why did the success of *CSI* seem uncertain before its premiere? To begin with, although the female lead, Marg Helgenberger, had won acclaim and an Emmy for her supporting role in *China Beach* (1988–91), and the male lead, William Petersen, had made something of a cultish name for himself from two offbeat crime films, *To Live and Die in LA* (1985) and *Manhunter* (1986), neither actor was a high-profile star with a history of carrying a TV series or headlining TV movies. Moreover, Anthony E. Zuiker, the creator of *CSI*, was an unknown and untested writer; a former tram driver at the Mirage Hotel in Las Vegas, he had reportedly got the idea for this new series from watching an episode of *The New Detectives: Case Studies in Forensic Science* (1996–2004) on the Discovery Channel.[2] Because of Zuiker's inexperience, Carol Mendelsohn and Ann Donahue were recruited to serve as co-executive producers with him. But while they had written for television, the two women did not have much of a background in the crime show genre: Mendelsohn, an inactive lawyer, had worked her way up the industry ranks from staff writer to co-executive producer of *Melrose Place* (1994–9); and Donahue had supervised two seasons of *Picket Fences* (1992–6). The pilot's British director, Danny Cannon, came to *CSI* with a background in action films, but his resumé, topped by *Judge Dredd* (1995) and *I Still Know What You Did Last Summer* (1998), gave no indication of the creativity he would bring to the series.

Perhaps the only truly bankable name attached to the project was Jerry Bruckheimer. His new TV production company, run on a day-to-day basis by its president, Jonathan Littman (who is another credited co-executive producer of *CSI* and all the Bruckheimer company's subsequent TV shows), would quickly make its mark on the medium almost simultaneously with *CSI* and *The Amazing Race* (2001–). At the time of *CSI*'s development, though, Bruckheimer had yet to transfer to television his savvy knack for making successful blockbuster action movies such as *Beverly Hills Cop* (1984), *Top Gun* (1985), *Armageddon* (1998) and *Enemy of the State* (1998).

Making the future prospects of *CSI* even more tenuous, several months before its premiere, the Canadian-owned Alliance Atlantis succeeded Disney's subsidiary unit, Touchstone Television, as a producing partner with CBS and Bruckheimer.[3] Touchstone unexpectedly withdrew from the new series because of doubts about its profitability, but also in order to preserve production-broadcasting synergy with Disney's competing ABC network, resulting in negative buzz about the forensic crime drama's potential.[4] It therefore came as a surprise when *CSI*'s share of the viewing audience was 'especially potent', as *Daily Variety* reported, with this new show delivering the best numbers for CBS on a Friday night in nearly a decade. 'If they hold up,' the trade paper observed, 'the numbers will sting execs at ABC/Touchstone, which developed the actioner.'[5]

Not only did the ratings hold up but, midway through the 2000–1 season, CBS moved *CSI* to Thursday in an effort to challenge NBC's long-standing control of the week's most profitable primetime night. This risky gamble paid off handsomely. CBS soon caught up with its rival, eventually taking over the night hands down three years later

The CSI team arrives at a crime scene

with its powerhouse trio of *Survivor* (2000–), *CSI* and *Without a Trace*
(2002–). But before that happened, as *CSI* itself reached number one in
the weekly ratings during its second season, CBS saw the series brand as
a lucrative franchise, leading to a successful spin-off set in Miami
(2002–) as the original began its third season, then to another one set in
New York City (2004–) as the original began its fifth season. Until ABC
moved its popular series *Grey's Anatomy* (2005–) opposite it in autumn
2007, *CSI* remained the top-rated scripted series on US television.

    CSI and its two spin-offs are just as popular globally.
The ratings of Five, the fifth and newest terrestrial TV channel in the
UK, owe much to the three series, so much so that in 2006 the network
inaugurated an online video on demand service featuring episodes for
paid download, with the most recent ones made available a week prior
to their broadcast in the UK.[6] On average, *CSI* draws well over three
million British viewers each week. It does about the same in each of the
large European nations. While less than that of the most popular
domestic programmes in the individual markets, such a sizeable
audience still ranks *CSI* among the most watched US television shows

around the world. In Asia, the *CSI* triple-header is a tent pole of Sony's AXN satellite network, 'the self-dubbed "Home of CSI"', which has 'a huge fan base of 25 million viewers' across the continent.[7]

Because of Bruckheimer's reputation as a film-maker, *CSI* immediately drew interest from international broadcasters when the series was previewed at MIPCOM, an annual TV trade show in Cannes.[8] The Miami spin-off, a more conventional action-driven show featuring an exotic tropical setting along with a more sentimentalised protagonist, has since eclipsed its source as the top-rated TV series in the global market according to Informa Telecoms and Media, which in 2006 listed *CSI* in sixth place.[9] However, despite the fresh competition from *Grey's Anatomy*, *CSI* continues to outperform its spin-offs and imitators in the USA, and as its ninth season approaches, it still serves as the anchor of CBS's primetime schedule.

Yet for all its popularity, *CSI* has not achieved high visibility as either a critical favourite or cult show. *CSI* resists the trend in serialised drama and strong, continuing character arcs that help to stimulate appointment television, Internet buzz and regular coverage in the entertainment press. 'It's not an Emmy darling, its cast isn't deemed "hot" or "hip" enough to make the cover of magazines, and it's not even the No. 1 drama on its night – but you won't find a hotter show on television,' *Daily Variety* noted as *CSI* reached twenty-five million viewers a week during its second season.[10] Six years later, despite a few awards and a long run as the top-rated show each week, that assessment more or less holds true.

CSI may therefore seem an unsuitable choice for inclusion in a line of books devoted to TV classics. It is a continuing series, whose mainstream success reflects the middlebrow tastes of commercial American television. For all its stylistic dazzle and high concept, *CSI* is genre television; and its genre, the crime show, is a long-standing and formulaic staple of primetime. Furthermore, the glitzy Las Vegas setting, emphasis on sex crimes and gruesome, CGI-enhanced dissecting and probing of body parts only make *CSI*'s appeal seem all the more superficial and escapist. Nonetheless, I believe that *CSI* is in its own right a

'TV classic'. If nothing else, its influence on contemporary US television was felt almost immediately. The show's success inspired numerous imitators on CBS, most produced under the Bruckheimer brand. In addition to the two bearing the series name, the others (*Without a Trace, NCIS* [2003–], *Cold Case* [2003–], *Numb3rs* [2005–], *et al.*) not only follow the procedural investigative format but also copy the visual style and attention to forensic science now considered a signature of the brand. Although other networks have followed suit (NBC's *Crossing Jordan* [2001–7], Fox's *Bones* [2005–]), a glance at its primetime schedule gives the impression that CBS stands for 'Crime Broadcasting System'.

From this perspective alone, *CSI* warrants serious attention. Moving its genre's terrain and focus away from the urban New York grittiness of *NYPD Blue* (1993–2005) on ABC or, more noticeably, the 'ripped from the headlines' banner of the long-running *Law and Order* (1990–) and its several branded spin-offs on NBC, *CSI* is responsible for the 21st-century reinvention of the crime show in terms of style and content. I shall elaborate later on, but put simply for the moment, the series refocuses around scientific investigation, and not, as on the *Law and Order* shows, the police or legal system, the genre's preoccupation with determining the truth of a crime as the condition enabling justice to prevail. For many critics of this decade's 'crime-time TV', the genre's revitalisation in the wake of *CSI*'s unexpected success is a post-September 11 phenomenon; it reaffirms the credibility and, hence, authority of state institutions (the police, the FBI, the CIA, the Office of Homeland Security, etc.) by offering an alternative means (science) of achieving a comforting ('true' *and* 'just'), not to say quick (in an hour's time), closure. The presumption, as one legal scholar remarks, is that 'the popularity of *CSI* lies in its ability to simplify the messy uncertainties of real-world crime'[11] – and by extension, when one considers the range of procedural crime dramas inspired by *CSI*, of scarier real-world global terrorism. However, as I shall be discussing throughout this book and want to emphasise, on *CSI*, in contrast with its imitators, it is rarely that simple.

Despite – or perhaps because of – both its undeniable influence on primetime television and its ideological currency, whenever I mention to someone that *CSI* is my own appointment show, the response – and not only from fellow academics – is usually wide-eyed surprise at my choice, followed by a frown ('much too gory and violent!') and the name of the other person's preference (invariably *Lost* [2004–] or *24* [2001–] or *The Sopranos* [1999–2007]). What do I find so compelling about *CSI* that makes me eagerly anticipate each new episode and, indeed, motivates me to write this book? I suppose the short answer is that *CSI* follows a group of obsessive intellectuals working collaboratively in a cloistered environment, not too different from my own professional life as a university professor, so it immediately encourages my identification each week with the characters' roles as interpreters of evidence. I seek the meaning in texts, and the forensic team members on *CSI* look for the same in the evidence they gather, in effect treating a crime scene as if it were a text.

But the long answer is that there is much more to *CSI* than that. Several key elements distinguish *CSI*, and although they overlap, this book will examine them more or less in sequence. These are:

1 the representation of forensic science as a correlative of truth and justice, which, in its coverage of 'The CSI Effect', the press claims works to mystify the unimpeachable clarity of evidence, although in the series itself ambiguity is as often the case;
2 the visual look of the series, from the stylised colour scheme to the 'CSI shots' that follow a bullet's trajectory through a victim's organs;
3 the narrative incorporation of Las Vegas's contrasting modern histories of gambling on the one hand and suburban expansion on the other; and
4 the thematic emphasis on social and sexual nonconformity, from the crimes being investigated in the iconic 'Sin City' locale to the characterisation of the forensic team as misfit intellectuals.

In the final analysis, I guess, my long answer as to what I find compelling about *CSI* will, as this book unfolds, turn out to be an elaboration of my short one.

6

1 It's All about the Evidence

As created by Anthony E. Zuiker, the premise of *CSI* is simple enough. Brilliant but eccentric scientist Gil Grissom (William Petersen), a world-famous entomologist, leads a team of smart, well-trained criminalists – Catherine Willows (Marg Helgenberger), Warrick Brown (Gary Dourdan), Nick Stokes (George Eads), Sara Sidle (Jorja Fox) and Greg Sanders (Eric Szmanda) – who work the graveyard shift in Las Vegas along with detective Jim Brass (Paul Guilfoyle), medical examiner Dr Al Robbins (Robert David Hall) and an assortment of recurring characters in the lab and the field. Although on occasion, a single crime requires the forensic team to work together, each weekly episode usually comprises two, sometimes three, plots involving the criminalists in varying combinations.

On the face of it, the science in *CSI* may seem to function simply as an excuse for the usual TV mix of sex and violence. Most episodes recount stories common enough for the crime show genre: cases having to do with murder, greed, domestic abuse, rape, sexual perversions, robbery, drugs, etc. The *CSI* twist on crime occurs with the revelation that its motivation can be as bizarre – or on occasion as benign – as its execution is gruesome. At the very least, either the teaser of an episode ('Lucky Strike' begins with a man speeding through the streets, chased by police, yet he falls out of his stopped car with a stake driven through his skull) or the conclusion ('Gentle, Gentle' reveals that the killer of an infant was his toddler sibling) will deliver the shock that has become a *CSI* signature. While often quite disturbing in their brutality and with unexpected turns throughout that cleverly, if unnervingly, surprise an audience, the crimes themselves, though, are shown retrospectively and even then only briefly. In the present tense of an episode's story, that of the forensic investigations, the team approaches the cases as riddles that their science solves. In the pilot, Catherine Willows says, 'I really love my job. We're just a bunch of kids that are getting paid to work on puzzles.' Eight years later, her excitement has not waned. Catherine, Grissom and the rest of the CSIs mouth commonplaces about catching 'the bad guys', but what obviously intrigues them most about their job is that a crime can be reconstructed and the perpetrator's identity discovered from minute traces left behind at the event.

Upon close inspection, in fact, much of the action occurring in any episode of *CSI* dramatises the forensic team's mundane labour: dusting for and lifting fingerprints, collecting hair samples, taking digital photos, testing surfaces for traces of human blood, observing an autopsy, swabbing for and then awaiting results of DNA, viewing surveillance videos, or, for that matter, breeding insects found on a corpse in order to ascertain time of death through 'linear regression'. This is all rather static activity by television standards – and a challenge to the actors' skills when playing such scenes. If members of the CSI team aren't talking to each other, ruminating aloud or interrogating someone, they perform their work in silence. *CSI* 'is a show about thinking and watching people think', Zuiker notes in one of his DVD commentaries ('Burked'). Outside the lab, team members arrive at or revisit crime scenes, accompany Brass or some other detective when tracking a suspect or issuing a search warrant, and that's about it. Unlike its spin-offs, the criminologists on *CSI* are not sworn police officers, although they carry guns, so this series rarely takes to the streets after 'the bad guys' in fast-paced action sequences.[12] *CSI* concentrates instead on the expertise, technology and mental work needed to solve crimes in the lab.[13]

8

Watching people think: the CSIs discuss a case, await DNA results, examine blood splatter marks

Because *CSI* redirects the crime show genre around 'the nerd squad', as a policeman refers to the team right off the bat in the pilot, the show's visual style compensates for its lack of conventional physical action. Enhanced close-ups, the now famous 'CSI shots', probe the interior of a body to illustrate the cause of death or display a specialised piece of hi-tech equipment in operation. Scenes in the lab and autopsy room are filmed in a colour palette dominated by cool blues in juxtaposition with warm shades of yellow for the desert climate of Las Vegas and the neon-like reds or greens of casinos and other nightspots. Either as visualisation of a witness's testimony or as a CSI's theory of what possibly happened, enactments of a crime occur many times in grainy or monochromatic flashbacks, often with off-centre camerawork and jerky editing. These stylistic techniques all make the otherwise static action of the forensic investigation more interesting to watch.

This distinctive *CSI* style visually parallels how the series's writers characterise the team leader Grissom in relation to his science. The chilly blue colouring of lab and autopsy scenes, almost antiseptic in their look, often feels like an extension of Grissom's commitment to the equally cold-hearted purity of science, which accounts for his aloofness. He projects a sense of being emotionally distant from the frenzied human desires that often lead to crime, clinically observing the world as a curious yet unobtrusive bystander who repeatedly lets the evidence 'speak for itself'. The chilly impersonality with which Grissom practises forensic science is further brought out by the many idiosyncrasies characterising his quirky brilliance: his knowledge about and comfort with insects, his rigorous intellectualism and sardonic but also whimsical sense of humour, his ability to absorb encyclopaedic knowledge like a sponge, his riding of roller-coasters and racing of cockroaches for relaxation, even his congenital hearing loss, which at times isolated him even from his team and was surgically corrected at the end of season three, yet still resonates in the show's use of silence.

Perhaps the most recognisable 'personal' note to Grissom's character is his unflagging loyalty to and patience with his co-workers.

He mentors as well as supervises them. They, in turn, view him as a role model, greatly respecting even while joking irreverently (though rarely to his face) about how far he will go in the interest of science. In 'Bodies in Motion', Greg accidentally gets a bit of goop from a liquefied corpse in his mouth. 'Technically that makes you a cannibal,' Sara comments, adding, 'Grissom would be proud.' Greg, who idolises him, corrects her: 'Grissom would've tasted it on purpose.'

One episode, 'Alter Boys', compares the purposeful science of Grissom, apparently an ex-Catholic, with a priest's faith. Faith requires trust in what cannot be proven empirically or logically, whereas science proves through empirical evidence and logical thought a form of knowledge one can trust with greater confidence. Indeed, whenever *CSI* teases viewers with possibilities of supernatural or paranormal phenomena, it ultimately accounts for them with scientific explanations, whether that means demystifying suspicions of vampirism ('Suckers'), lycanthropy ('Werewolves'), extraterrestrial aliens ('Viva Las Vegas', 'Leapin' Lizards') or birth by immaculate conception ('Secrets and Flies'). Nor is Grissom's science itself a form of illusion or trickery, even though it can confuse juries, as he is sometimes warned. Science is not 21st-century magic, notwithstanding the paradox that it is visualised for audiences of *CSI* by the computer wizardry of CGI artists. A conversation with a master illusionist in 'Abra-Cadaver' clarifies that, whereas magic plays upon a confusion of seeming and knowing, science does just the opposite:

ZEPHYR: Nothing is as it seems, is it?
GRISSOM: That's the conflict of magic – the burden of knowledge versus the mystique of wonder.
ZEPHYR: And you're wondering right now – I can hear your mind ticking – 'Was she a plant? Was it real?'
GRISSOM: Well, there are no secrets, are there? Only hidden answers.
ZEPHYR: I'm an honest liar, sir. In my line of work it's accepted. You could say it was my livelihood.
GRISSOM: Well, my livelihood is dispelling lies and finding the truth.

11

In portraying Grissom and his team as crime solvers 'finding the truth' and not as crime fighters imposing the law – in short, as forensic scientists only – *CSI* significantly differs from the series cloned in its image, where investigators use science but are, first and foremost, police officers or their federal counterparts. I think this difference is crucial, beginning with the characterisation of Grissom as a brilliant yet eccentric scientist.

For a simple illustration, consider how *CSI* stands apart from its imitators by the way it closes its teasers, a well-worn convention of the crime show genre for revealing a crime scene, depicting the arrival of series regulars, then segueing to the opening credits. The *CSI: Miami* forensic team supervisor, police lieutenant Horatio Caine (David Caruso), ends a teaser with a pseudo-aphorism meant to warn whoever committed the crime that he will deliver justice. With dark sunglasses shielding his eyes from the Miami sun but also obscuring the direction of his gaze in order to emphasise his authority, Caine speaks with an overstated sense of self-importance. Although he heads the Miami CSI unit and knows the science, Caine's authority comes from his identification with the law, which is also why this series characterises him as the protector of helpless women and innocent children. In *CSI*, the more intellectual and emotionally aloof Grissom, almost always more interested in the evidence than in the suspects themselves as he readily admits, ends a teaser on a wry, ironical note. Grissom quotes Shakespeare or Edgar Allen Poe with tongue in cheek, makes a joke that cleverly plays on a well-worn phrase or cliché, or responds to the enigma of a crime scene with whimsical understatement. When confronted with a missing person in 'Chaos Theory', detective Brass says gruffly, 'One moment Paige Rycoff is here, the next ... vanished,' to which Grissom retorts, 'People don't vanish, Jim. It's a molecular impossibility.' Cut to The Who performing the *CSI* theme song, Pete Townshend's 'Who Are You?'.

The reluctance to sentimentalise Grissom in the teasers, in contrast with how *CSI: Miami* uses Caine, keeps attention focused on Grissom's role as a scientist and not a cop; his official, not to say intellectual and emotional, distance from the institution of policing

12

William Petersen as Gil Grissom

prevents his science from being co-opted by the law and the ideological purposes served by television's representations of cops as symbolic figures of male authority, well typified by Caine. For the same reason, as in the teasers, throughout an episode of *CSI* Grissom's wry sense of irony often supplies the line of dialogue that punctuates a cut to the next scene or a commercial break, his perspective thereby guiding the punchy, fast-moving pace of the editing.

13

CSI is just as reticent to sentimentalise (some may say 'fetishise') the state apparatus of law and order, as most other shows in the genre have done in response to the cultural anxieties about national security following the events of September 11. While it may be due to the fact that *CSI* was conceived of and began to air before then, the singularity of this series in refraining from making such a simplistic move on its part still holds. *Without a Trace*, for several seasons the companion series of *CSI* on Thursday evening in the USA, asks us to imagine the FBI as a missing-persons bureau, the well-intending instrument of a benevolent state that rescues people from themselves. By contrast, *CSI* is often suspicious of and on occasion downright antagonistic to the legal and governmental institutions guaranteeing law and order. Instead of resorting to the reassuring sentimentality that characterises its spin-offs or imitators, *CSI* reiterates in episode after episode the maxim, 'People lie. The evidence doesn't lie' ('Crate 'n' Burial'). The forensic team must disregard the people involved in a crime except as sources of telling dishonesty and instead be impartially analytical in its investigations. 'We don't crunch the evidence to fit a theory,' Grissom reminds Sara in 'Sex, Lies and Larvae'.

  CSI reinforces the impersonality of science by exploiting its tension with the law as rival guarantors of 'truth' and 'justice'. Friction arising between science and law manifests itself most openly in the professional clashes between Grissom, who refuses to sacrifice the scientific integrity of his investigations, and his politically minded boss Conrad Ecklie (Marc Vann), the Clark County sheriff and undersheriff, the mayor of Las Vegas, antagonistic cops resenting the team's intrusion, and various defence attorneys and prosecutors. Such eruptions of disobedience and disrespect on Grissom's part serve to quash any speculation that economic self-interest motivates the criminologists, even though they are, after all, working for the city, serving the police and providing the DA with the means to go to trial. The series posits that, in its impartiality, a bona fide forensic investigation is above politics, unable to make the evidence deliver what someone outside the lab may want it to say.

  A few episodes directly address the concern, otherwise countered by Grissom's refusal to submit to his superiors, that science can manipulate evidence to serve any number of interests. In 'The Accused Is Entitled', Grissom goes against his former mentor, hired by a movie star's ruthless defence attorney to discredit the lab's findings in a speedy preliminary hearing. Since the evidence against the star cannot be attacked – he's been caught in lies, has blood on his hands, etc. – the team's method of collecting evidence is made the target. One by one, a criminalist's testimony is twisted so that his or her credibility casts doubt on the evidence presented to the presiding judge. 'It's not what did happen,' the former mentor states to Nick in Grissom's presence. 'It's what a jury believes could have happened.' Opposing the cynicism of such 'a bottom feeder', Grissom reminds his team that 'CSI's always on trial ... The burden of truth is on us.' Likewise, in 'Secrets and Flies', at the request of the undersheriff (who has a personal interest in the case), Grissom goes up against a former collaborator. Now 'a gun for hire', an expert witness hired by the defence to disprove through 'linear regression' the prosecution's timeline of the crime, this scientist rigs his lab findings in order to earn his large salary and to sustain his inflated reputation. 'Well, I've seen him on the stand,' Catherine comments. 'He manipulates evidence.' 'He manipulates people,' Grissom responds. 'The public assumes that scientists are ethical, but many of us are no better than politicians, evidently.'

The rival experts in these two episodes sell out their science for profit, abusing its methodology and purpose, and in both cases Grissom's own impartiality does hold up to 'the burden of truth'. In order to drive home the point that his science remains uncompromised by economic or political self-interest, when the undersheriff says he owes Grissom a favour at the close of 'Secrets and Flies', all the scientist asks for is to have his tardy personnel evaluations backdated so that his team can get their full merit raises.

In still another episode, Grissom tells the producer of a TV reality show, 'the truth is if there isn't any evidence we have nowhere to go'. The producer then asks if 'forensic shows are teaching the criminals how to get away with crimes'. Grissom answers, 'Everyone learns from science. It all depends on how you use the knowledge' ('I Like to Watch'). Science, as opposed to the uses to which it is put, is inherently unbiased and thus unimpeachable as the source of irrefutable evidence. Nor is science an abstraction; rather, its concreteness provides the basis of 'knowledge' for practitioners with integrity and intellect like Grissom, so pursuing this 'knowledge' is made tantamount to 'finding truth', regardless of whether truth is plain as day, hidden by subterfuge or made evident in microscopic particles.

For all its obvious endorsement of scientific objectivity, *CSI* nonetheless complicates this premise by framing it through two lead characters, with the more subjective perspective represented by Catherine Willows placed alongside the objective one of Grissom.

15

Marg Helgenberger as Catherine Willows

16   When he asks Catherine why she is attending the execution of a man
whom her forensic findings helped to convict – it will be her first
personal encounter with the death penalty – she replies, 'It's like your
first autopsy . . . your first murdered child. You can make it through that
you can keep doing this work.' For his part, Grissom holds up the results
of a paint sample comparison: 'See, being capable of matching paint
samples that are fifteen years apart – that's why I keep doing this work.'
Smiling, Catherine observes, 'Well, that's the difference between you and
me' ('The Execution of Catherine Willows').

Catherine is perhaps the feistiest member of the CSI team:
she is hard-talking, assertive and sexually frank; unafraid to get dirty on
the job, which she clearly enjoys and is good at; came to her career the
hard way by taking night classes at the local university; and is
unashamed of her previous occupation as an 'exotic dancer', which, she
tells the defence attorney in 'The Accused Is Entitled', paid '*very* well'.
Respecting Grissom as a peer, Catherine is the only member of the CSI
team who does not look up to him as her mentor, so she rarely shies

away from telling him what's on her mind, whether to argue with him about a case or to point out his failings as an administrator.

Catherine's and Grissom's often contrasting behaviour both as professionals and individuals complements but also tests the other's limits. If she gets too close to a case, he pulls her back. By the same token, her subjectivity can expose the myopia resulting from his objectivity, which makes him fail to appreciate except on an intellectual level (and thus be 'deaf' to) unpredictable human emotions. In 'Face Lift', a murder investigation ends up locating a young woman, long presumed to be dead, who as a child had been abducted from her parents. Grissom arranges for the couple to see their daughter from afar and is surprised when the mother tries to make contact, causing a commotion. 'What were you thinking?' Catherine asks. Grissom can only sigh: 'I don't know. I wanted to observe, I guess.'

CATHERINE: That woman hasn't seen her daughter in twenty-one years. You actually thought a glass wall would keep them apart?
GRISSOM: I never thought about that.
CATHERINE: I know. You're not good with people.
GRISSOM: Yeah.

Catherine's perspective brings out the naivety, at least when it comes to messy human responses, of Grissom's intellectual approach to science. This is not to say that Grissom never makes an emotional connection with a case. He becomes unusually obsessed with solving a murder in 'Butterflied' because of the victim's resemblance to Sara, with whom he has engaged in an enigmatic sexual flirtation from the series' start. Nor is he himself immune to human error. A case comes to a dead end midway through 'Sex, Lies and Larvae' because of a mistake he makes in calculating time of death through insect maturation. Only after a frustrated and angry Sara reveals that she is haunted at night by the victim's cries does Grissom repeat his test, this time by adding a factor to his experiment that he had not thought of previously (the fact that the victim was tightly bound up in a blanket, which retarded the flies'

Catherine asks Grissom, 'What were you thinking?'

entrance into her body). But even then he tells Brass that it is people who make mistakes, not the insects – or the science behind 'linear regression'.

18   Grissom's inability to fathom unpredictable emotions, evident in 'Face Lift' when the mother's action takes him by surprise, never seriously challenges his objectivity, however. While their different talents productively mesh, Grissom's impersonal scientific view usually trumps Catherine's interpersonal skills. Along with her greater sensitivity to people as people and not specimens, she is the one *CSI* character with a strong continuing backstory involving her daughter, ex-husband and familial relation to old-school casino tycoon, Sam Braun (Scott Wilson). While this extended backstory gives Catherine a fully rounded characterisation – making her perhaps the richest and most varied member of the entire *CSI* team, surely the one with the most thoroughly dramatised private life – it puts a strain on her scientific impartiality.

      Despite her own undeniable expertise and professionalism as a criminalist, whenever backstory becomes a plot issue Catherine's personal involvement in a case jeopardises its outcome, most notably so when she uses blood evidence to find out if Sam Braun is her biological father ('Inside the Box') and her actions result in the case against Braun for murder getting thrown out of court ('Assume Nothing'). In other episodes, Catherine, ignoring Grissom's warning, investigates when her ex-husband is charged with rape ('Who Are You?'); accepts a large monetary gift for her daughter from Braun, which can be construed as a bribe ('Jackpot'); meddles in Sara's investigation of a car crash involving both her daughter, who nearly drowns, and her ex-husband, who has gone missing and later turns up dead ('Lady Heather's Box'); causes an explosion in the lab that destroys DNA evidence and injures Greg ('Play with Fire'); and is hit on while unwinding at a bar by a man who gets furious because she turns him down and whom she later goes after too zealously when circumstances point to him as the most likely suspect in a murder ('Weeping Willows'). Additionally, on two occasions her own body becomes evidence, first when a suspect attacks her and flees a crime scene ('A Little Murder'), and second when she is drugged and set up to think she has been raped in a motel, part of a vengeance scheme directed at Braun that ends with his dying in her arms outside a casino ('Built to Kill, Part Two').

By contrast, backstory for the rest of the team, including Grissom, only emerges in bits and pieces, often in humorous throwaway dialogue while they work. These exchanges give Greg the opportunity for disclosing his many quirky interests and for talking about his equally peculiar Scandinavian grandfather; likewise, through casual conversation Warrick learns that Grissom financed his first body farm while in college by playing competitive poker ('Revenge Is Best Served Cold'). Or an episode briefly introduces backstory to account for professional motivation, explaining, albeit several seasons later, Sara's obsessive drive when it comes to cases of spousal abuse of the sort that haunts her in 'Sex, Lies and Larvae'. On the few occasions when backstory does more than that – when Warrick's gambling addiction or inner-city childhood, say, becomes an operative factor in a case – as with Catherine's backstory, its plot prominence troubles the character's objectivity. Investigating a drive-by shooting that causes the death of his mentor's young daughter, Warrick is blindsided by his bias and it results in an innocent man's brutalisation ('Random Acts of Violence').

19

Paul Guilfoyle as Captain Jim Brass

George Eads as Nick Stokes

Gary Dourdan as Warrick Brown

Jorja Fox as Sara Sidle

Eric Szmanda as Greg Sanders

Robert David Hall as Dr Al Robbins

Even Grissom's hearing loss, which deprives him of the full sensory input needed for his work and which he has kept hidden at the risk of isolating him from his team, becomes a liability for his science when it goes beyond serving as a character note. His mentor, who deduces it from his first-hand knowledge of Grissom's family medical history, tries to exploit the impairment in 'The Accused Is Entitled'.

Generally speaking, *CSI* focuses on the evidence through the central difference between Grissom and Catherine as it emerges out of their contrasting characterisations and the prominence or marginality of their backstories. On one hand, we see the mind in action. This is what forensic science makes evident when it solves an inscrutable crime through disciplined and logical reasoning, and it is what Grissom's aloof stance as a scientist, not to mention his eccentric brilliance, personifies. Yet in their subtle execution, many crimes imply a comparable intellectual at work, too. On the other hand, we see desire in action. This is what the crimes more obviously make manifest, so in this regard desire contextualises forensic science's object of study. Yet desire is also what Catherine's viewpoint and backstory incorporate into the investigations in order to temper the scientist's potential for being estranged from humanity. Placed in tension with its counterpart, each perspective presses against the other's assumptions to define what science means and how it operates. Catherine takes into account the subjective basis of truth but without disqualifying scientific objectivity, just as Grissom always finds most intriguing the crimes that push beyond the limits of normalcy.

The lead characters of Gil Grissom and Catherine Willows work together in *CSI* to put a human face on the science. More importantly, their two perspectives function in conjunction to keep in place the stability of evidence as the proper object of scientific inquiry so that its objectivity quite literally remains firmly vested in the object – the evidence – and not the person. As Grissom tells Catherine in 'Bloodlines': 'You can be wrong, I can be wrong, the evidence is just the evidence.'

2 The *CSI* Effect

Given how this series uses science to determine the characters, the action, the visuals and the objectivity of evidence, it's not surprising that science takes centre stage whenever the press writes about *CSI*.[14] The production company exploits such coverage, publicising the crime-lab setting by licensing toy *CSI* forensic kits, for instance, or working with Chicago's Museum of Science and Industry on an interactive exhibit, *CSI: The Experience*. This exhibit, 'where visitors can gather evidence, run tests and crack the case just like the investigators do on the show',[15] addresses an issue raised by the press about the series, namely, its 'realism', though I doubt if audiences take *CSI* entirely at face value.

Certainly, in an episode's foreshortening of the time required for processing and receiving results, one ought to recognise the convention of hour-long drama that accounts for a necessary lack of fidelity to real-life forensic labour. The series compresses duration through montages showing one of the CSIs or lab techs patiently waiting for a hit on CODIS (Combined DNA Index System) or AFIS (Automated Fingerprint Identification System) or painstakingly analysing debris from an explosion or dumpster. Receipt of DNA testing or requisition of telephone records can take months, not hours, in real-life time, whereas it's all in a day's work on *CSI*. More noteworthy to the press is the questionable accuracy of the technology as well as methods used in the *CSI* lab. Some of the highly sophisticated and innovative machinery and computer software can be found in real-life forensic laboratories but are often too expensive for real labs to purchase, while some do not yet exist, at least not to the extent shown on the series.[16]

The cohort of *CSI* writers makes good use of technical advisers, with 'over 400 expert contacts throughout the criminal justice, law enforcement, forensics, and medical communities, whom they rely on to answer technical questions related to the show'.[17] David Berman, who plays David Phillips, the assistant medical examiner, is the lead researcher, assisted by Jon Wellner, also cast as one of the many lab techs, Henry Andrews; and Elizabeth Devine, a former criminalist initially hired to advise writers, became story editor and then began writing scripts herself.

For all the research, though, at times the series abandons realism for the sake of good television. Midway through 'Bodies in Motion', police notice an abandoned automobile with a powerful stench. Inside the trunk, Grissom and Sara find two decayed, soupy corpses, so he orders the vehicle to be wrapped in sheets of thin plastic to preserve evidence before it gets transported back to the lab. 'Car condom', Grissom jokes. An audacious image with a funny punchline, no? But to motivate it, the script conveniently ignores that in real life plastic wrap contaminates trace evidence, effacing or disturbing fingerprints, DNA, gunshot residue and bloodstains. Grissom's 'car condom' will therefore render the car pretty useless by the time it reaches the lab. Rick Workman, a real-life CSI first in Las Vegas and now in neighbouring Henderson, served as one of Anthony Zuiker's initial consultants, and he recalls phoning Jon Wellner immediately after this episode aired in order to ask, what *were* the writers thinking? 'Dave [Berman] and I told them you wouldn't like it,' Wellner laughed, adding that even on *CSI* technical accuracy must sometimes take a back seat to 'entertainment and visual appeal'.[18]

Because scientific fact and fiction can so easily commingle in *CSI*, the press has most repeatedly discussed what it calls 'The *CSI* Effect', using the phrase to depict two separate phenomena. First, 'The *CSI* Effect' refers to the sudden popularity of forensic science courses in colleges nationwide as a result of *CSI*'s glamorising of the profession, much as *L.A. Law* (1986–94) appeared to increase enrolments in law schools and *ER* (1994–) in medical schools. Second and more commonly, 'The *CSI* Effect' refers to the concern that *CSI*'s attention to forensic science has resulted in real-life juries unrealistically expecting definitive DNA and similar trace evidence at every trial. The claim being made is that the popularity of *CSI* has led to a rise in jury acquittals. Most prosecution cases usually do not need DNA or other trace testing; they already have enough traditional evidence to go to trial without resorting to the expense of *CSI*-styled findings, too, yet the series has supposedly convinced juries to have 'reasonable doubt' whenever such forensic tests are not offered as evidence.

Scholars are unsure whether or not a '*CSI* Effect' is indeed verifiable. According to legal scholar Tom R. Tyler, 'there is little objective evidence demonstrating that the effect exists', only anecdotal accounts offered by unhappy prosecutors trying to explain a jury decision that has gone against them.[19] Indeed, Tyler puts forward an equally persuasive hypothesis that 'The *CSI* Effect' facilitates rather than impedes affirmative jury decisions. Forensic evidence, he reasons, can 'overweigh the probative value of science, putting a greater weight on such evidence than its statistical value warrants'. Tyler speculates that, as a consequence and just as they do on television, scientific findings provide jurors with an easier means of legitimating difficult convictions because the forensic proof fulfils the same desire for justice that crime shows like *CSI* satisfy.[20] Either way, scholars examining a possible '*CSI* Effect' on juries consider it a media invention, on a par with 'The *Perry Mason* Effect' during that series's run (1957–66), which, it was believed, caused juries to expect a last-minute confession on the witness stand at each and every trial.

A more profound way to think about 'The *CSI* Effect', though, is to frame it through this question: What are the *ideological* consequences arising from an endorsement of science that simultaneously cautions an audience to disregard the value of eye-witness accounts and to trust instead only forensic findings? *CSI* fosters its premise, as another legal scholar, Michael D. Mann, puts it, 'that the

25

only reliable proof is scientific evidence' in the various ways it
distinguishes science from the law as the more objective and hence
credible means of finding truth and enacting justice.[21] *CSI* does so as
well by having someone declare in episode after episode that science
supersedes witness accounts even on the rare occasion when the account
proves true. As Grissom explains to one suspect, whom he happens to
believe in this instance, 'We're trained to ignore verbal accounts and rely
instead on the evidence a scene sets before us' ('Cool Change').
The presumption of science's veracity and, conversely, of speech's
unreliability in itself amounts to a view of the world that is ideological
because it treats science as a language in its own right – as a means of
formulating, perceiving and understanding 'truth' as the path to
'justice'. I have been paying such close attention to the CSI team's own
articulations of their science's value for this very reason.

Taking the roles of both prosecution and defence when
examining the numerous possibilities by which a '*CSI* Effect' can be
construed, Tyler points out the issue at the heart of the debate. 'The legal
system', he observes, 'must confront two interrelated objects: truth and
justice. Truth is the prerequisite for justice; without knowing the facts of
the case it is impossible to determine whether justice has been done.'[22]
In the Miami spin-off, as in the many other procedural crime shows on

US television right now, forensic science discloses truth in the interest of justice because the investigations occur in the name of the state's legal system. The investigators may use science to break a case but they carry badges to arrest the criminals, bringing them to justice. If the legal system, both in its own right and as an institution of the state, has lost credibility for the viewing public, then a series like *CSI: Miami* restores the system's authority by making sure that the law exposes truth in order to deliver justice; the science is a means to that greater end. This underlying ideological view of the state justly serving its citizens accounts for the benevolent view of the legal system as an institution that saves people in peril and, given the corruption existing outside of it (for *CSI: Miami* this corruption takes the form of drug cartels, gun-runners, terrorist cells and self-indulgent billionaires), that restores social order to the best of it abilities. It also accounts for the sentimental characterisation of Horatio Caine as a lone police hero and not a forensic team member, as a man with a badge and not an academic reputation; in short, as the very opposite of Gil Grissom.

When, on the other hand, *CSI* posits the impartial accuracy of forensic science in probing evidence, this series voices a different ideological view of truth and justice. *CSI* treats forensic methods as evidentiary facts, but the principles motivating and disciplining the

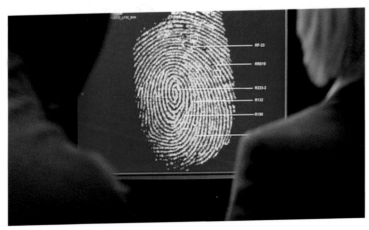

investigators' work are not 'facts'. In other words, forensic *theory*, the basis of most evidence testing by criminalists, is taken to be forensic *truth* on *CSI*. In a *New Yorker* article comparing the forensic science on the show with that of real-life criminalists, Jeffrey Toobin, also the senior legal analyst on CNN, reports:

> Virtually all the forensic-science tests depicted on 'CSI' – including analyses of bite marks, blood spatter, handwriting, firearm and tool marks, and voices, as well as of hair and fibers – rely on the judgments of individual experts and cannot easily be subjected to statistical verification.

Toobin quotes one professor who calls DNA 'real science' and most other forensic testing 'faith-based science'. 'There is no scientific evidence, no validation studies, or anything else that scientists usually demand, for that proposition – that, say, two hairs that look alike came from the same person,' this expert states. 'It's the individualization fallacy, and it's not real science.'[23]

Toobin's point is not to discredit hair or any other type of trace analysis, since it does provide a very useful starting point for building a case; but he does caution against elevating the value of forensic findings beyond their theoretical application. And Toobin is not alone. In his lengthy analysis of the '*CSI* Effect', Michael D. Mann similarly comments, 'all that is clear about scientific evidence is that scientific evidence is not clear'.[24] Placing hair analysis on the same level as DNA and at the expense of witness testimony results in what Mann and other scholars call 'junk science' – when forensic analysis claims, and leads jurors to believe, that its findings are more statistically certain (as opposed to statistically probable) than their verification can support.[25] Forensic scientists seem aware of a need to be cautious, too. Toobin interviews a New York counterpart of *CSI*'s Catherine Willows, who tells him that the language used in articulating forensic findings is crucial. 'On TV, they always like to say words like "match," but we say "similar," or "could have come from" or "is associated with".'[26]

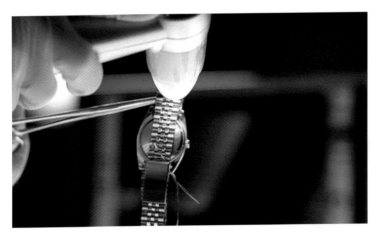

If it is not clear by this point, let me confess that my own interest when watching *CSI* has little to do with the accuracy or not of its science. But as should also be clear by now, I am fascinated by the way *CSI* represents forensic science as a set of values related to truth and justice. The show's criminalists repeatedly say that they are the only ones left to speak for the victims, to bring them justice. And if it is indeed all about the evidence, more careful study of the series makes evident just how vexing can be the pursuit of truth and justice through science, more so than the commentary about 'The *CSI* Effect' assumes when it critiques the series for endorsing 'junk science'.

29

The criminalists on *CSI* readily acknowledge that their task requires interpretative judgments about the evidence as informed by their training and experience. In 'The Execution of Catherine Willows', the defence attorney (Viola Davis) for a man on death row accuses Catherine of bias:

> ATTORNEY: You CSIs are biased for the prosecution. You decide ahead of time how you want the evidence to come out.
> CATHERINE: Ms Campbell, I am only an interpreter of the evidence. I know how to make the evidence speak to me. I don't care about the outcome.

Catherine's response typifies the series's evasiveness whenever it
approaches that grey area raised by Toobin's article – namely,
the question of *how* she hears the evidence speak to her – because we
are encouraged to believe that the method of her analysis itself plays no
significant role in determining the meaning she finds there. It's just a
matter of applying science, right? The mediation of Catherine's 'hearing'
by scientific technology, like that of all the CSIs, helps to authenticate
her interpretation as straightforward, as discovery of a meaning
unaffected by theoretical hypotheses or even her own desire to convict.
For the technology, shown in all its bells and whistles and even given its
own unique perspective in the CSI shots, visually places her
interpretative 'hearing' at one remove from the evidence. It is the
scientific apparatus that gives the evidence its voice, not Catherine
herself. All she has to do is listen carefully so that she 'hears' the hidden
meaning.

At the same time, however, Catherine's statement beclouds the
premise that the meaning of evidence is, well, so very self-evident to the
trained investigator. For what does she have in mind when she refers to
not caring 'about the outcome'? That her science simply and impartially

30

Catherine defends the status of evidence to a zealous defence attorney

concerns itself with disclosing 'truth', regardless of who the finger of guilt points to, so that 'justice' follows automatically and without a need for additional interpretation, i.e. judgment at a trial? Possibly. After all, Grissom closes the teaser to this episode by reminding her, 'It's just about evidence. It's not up to you whether he lives or dies. Case has no face.' On the other hand, could Catherine and Grissom both be thinking that 'justice' – the later work of jury deliberation and the doling out of punishment by a judge – is a secondary stage of interpreting the evidence that occurs beyond the province of their scientific inquiry? If so, this in turn raises a possibility that, since it does not necessarily speak to justice, forensic science may ultimately be uncertain, too, at least uncertain enough to require that Catherine act as an 'interpreter' of the evidence, as she tells the attorney, to begin with.

I am not trying to overly complicate Catherine's statement in order to play devil's advocate. *CSI* itself raises questions about the density of evidence and, correspondingly, about the transparency that forensic science claims for it. Sometimes directly, sometimes indirectly, the series interrogates what the science brings to the evidence table as the truths of a case so that justice may – or possibly may not – be well served.

For an example, consider what happens in 'Invisible Evidence'. This episode opens with a judge ruling that a bloody knife with additional trace evidence, found in the defendant's car, is inadmissible, hence legally 'invisible'. Warrick Brown had collected the knife without first confirming if the police officer at the scene had a search warrant, and it is revealed at trial that the cop had neglected to request one, although he blames Warrick for the halt in the proceedings. Before freeing the defendant, the judge gives the CSI team twenty-four hours to prepare all the admissible evidence in the case, some of which it had been unnecessary to process fully before this time because of the knife's prominence. Going back over the remaining evidence, Warrick discovers that the wrong person is on trial, the bloody knife be damned. It was planted in the car by the real murderer, so the weapon deceptively pointed to the wrong man even when tested properly.

31

Evidence, in short, needs to be interpreted 'in context', as the CSIs sometimes put it, which now occurs as the case is revised and justice, in the determination of innocence and guilt *before* trial, can prevail as the science's outcome. The need to see the evidence in its full context is the reason why the team will hypothetically act out a crime, as they do in 'Chaos Theory' and 'Unfriendly Skies', or lay out the trajectory of multiple bullets with lasers, as in 'Paper or Plastic?', or revisit a crime scene in order to contextualise a piece of evidence, to see it in its 'natural habitat', as Sara puts it in 'The Hunger Artist'.

In 'I Like to Watch', an episode of season six built around awareness of the media's coverage of 'The *CSI* Effect', Brass tells the reality TV producer, 'Look, juries love explanations; they want it nice and neat. They don't want to know we live in a random world; they want meaning. It's that simple.' Science may even theorise the randomness Brass alludes to, but the theory offers cold comfort if justice is the only desired end. Grissom states in the teaser to 'Chaos Theory' that it is 'a molecular impossibility' that people vanish, and according to the laws of physics he is obviously correct. In this case, though, when the team has 'tons of motive' yet 'not a stitch of evidence', the solution to Paige Rycoff's disappearance resists the linear logic that otherwise structures *CSI* investigations. Not until Grissom realises he and his team must turn to 'Chaos Theory, random events, wholesale rejection of linear thought' can they figure out that Paige is dead and that this fatality resulted from 'a confluence of unrelated, unfortunate events'. To my mind, that is another way of saying that the evidence needs to be put in context and then interpreted for it to be understood.

When Grissom tells the parents (Garrett M. Brown and Sherry Hursey) 'no one is guilty of this', they persist in thinking, 'no, no, no. Somebody is responsible.' He confronts them with the intellectual gap, on the one hand, between the CSI team's hypothesis, which the criminalists reach only after acting out the events and discovering that nothing hangs together linearly, and, on the other hand, the desired concrete proof leading Mr and Mrs Rycoff to a sense of justice as compensation for their loss. The Rycoffs, in other words, want the

Following chaos theory, Grissom and the CSIs discover Paige Rycoff's body in the dumpster outside her college dormitory

evidence, which Grissom has previously informed them was their only connection to their missing daughter, to tell a story of causation and agency. Questions of linear causality leading back to a human agent – 'somebody is responsible' – therefore remain unanswered for the parents, who intend to pursue the matter by hiring a private investigator.

For Grissom, by contrast, chaos theory *is* the proof and hence the truth, a means of putting together the otherwise unrelated traces left by Paige's disappearance. 'We told them what happened,' he says to Catherine afterwards.

> CATHERINE: Yeah, but we didn't give them what they needed – some closure.
> GRISSOM: Truth brings closure.
> CATHERINE: Not always.

This conversation calls to mind the similar one in 'Face Lift' but also anticipates Brass's remark in 'I Like to Watch'. The detective's complaint about the 'nice and neat' explanations that juries 'want' in order to simplify their world applies as aptly to the clear-cut explanations that

33

the victim's parents seek in 'Chaos Theory'. Scholars like Tyler and Mann attribute the immense appeal of *CSI* to the same desire on the part of viewers to find a simpler world of truth and justice confirmed by the end of each hour-long episode. I won't deny that many viewers may well watch *CSI* to find that satisfaction, but this expectation should not obscure the frequency with which the series raises doubts about the ability of science to provide a truth that leads to legal or moral justice through a 'nice and neat' closure.

The first of the very few story arcs on *CSI* – 'Pilot' and 'Anonymous' in season one, 'Identity Crisis' in season two, the three episodes involving serial killer Paul Millander (Matt O'Toole) – establishes a breach between science and justice early on in the series's run. In 'Anonymous', Millander pays a bum to flip several pages of symbolic drawings before the camera of an ATM, and Grissom, Catherine and Sara interpret the filmed message as a declaration that the killer is seeking peace of mind. 'What do you have to attain to have peace of mind?' Catherine asks and immediately realises the answer is 'justice'. Grissom then interprets the full message to read: 'I'm going to keep doing this over and over again until I get justice.' This message makes justice and closure equivalent terms.

Before disappearing, Millander then leaves two additional messages that widen the gap between Grissom's sense of scientific truth as a form of closure in its own right and the justice Millander seeks. Grissom, Catherine, Brass and the police arrive at Millander's empty warehouse to find a blank sheet of paper that signifies that Grissom has nothing on him; meanwhile, Millander shows up at the forensic unit to wave into the surveillance camera at the entrance, asking the receptionist to tell Mr Grissom that 'a friend' stopped by to see him. This episode therefore ends with the truth of Millander's criminality fully evident to Grissom but with justice for the crimes deferred. If justice is the goal of forensic science, then Grissom's truth yields nothing but a blank page, which may be Millander's point.

To Grissom's utter surprise, in the following season the elusive serial killer reappears out of the blue as a Clark County judge dispensing justice in 'Identity Crisis', and he has Grissom arrested for contempt of court. Millander's story as it unfolds in this episode is too complicated to reiterate here, so I'll only point out in broad strokes how it picks up from 'Anonymous'. Grissom uses science to prove that Millander and the judge are one and the same, but Millander escapes from the courthouse while awaiting arraignment. Both judge and serial murderer, Millander executes justice himself by killing his mother and committing suicide before Grissom can realise that this is why he has escaped from the courthouse. Yet in escaping, Millander also does not want to elude Grissom; rather, he performs his act of justice with Grissom as his intended audience. Millander knows full well that the scientist will follow his tracks to his mother's house, where an audio tape has recorded the suicide. In completing this story arc, Millander himself provides the closure promised by justice, leaving science and its truth out of the loop. The episode ends with Grissom flinching at the sound of the recorded gunshot.

The Millander story arc is just one instance of how closure, especially when equated with a sense of a case's just ending, does not function all that nicely or neatly on *CSI* to equate 'truth' and 'justice', which is the point made by Brass's comment in 'I Like to Watch'. As in 'Chaos Theory', it probably goes without saying that this state of affairs happens as a matter of course if the crime turns out to be accidental. However, the limited satisfaction of scientific truth serving as its own reward is further implied when, as is the custom of this series, an episode closes without indicating the outcome, leaving open the question of whether the subtleties of a CSI's case will legally hold up to make an arrest stick or to convince a jury should the case go to trial.

As already stated, *CSI* has little interest in the institutions of law and order except when it gets in the way of the science. But aside from that disinterest, recall the many episodes that, with the open-endedness of cases in the finale, directly pressure the just closure promised by science's delivery of truth. The illusionist who murdered his sister and son escapes from police custody in the last moments of 'Abra-Cadaver'. He has one more trick up his sleeve (or in his mouth) that

Paul Millander

Millander sends his message about justice via the homeless man

Grissom, Catherine and Brass arrive at Millander's empty warehouse

Millander sends a friendly greeting to Grissom on the surveillance camera

A year later Millander returns as Judge Douglas Mason

. . . and Grissom is surprised to find him in the courtroom

Grissom thinks he has anticipated but hasn't fully figured out. The thieves in 'Suckers' perform a con game that, with the collected evidence continually changing its face, unfolds like nesting Russian dolls. By the time Grissom realises how they have stolen the ten million dollars from the casino's vault, the theatrical troupe have departed for parts unknown, leaving behind the manager who master-minded this convoluted and very clever robbery of his own establishment. He boasts that Grissom has nothing but 'notions', which is true as far as the evidence goes, so all the scientist can do in retaliation is threaten to pass on his findings to the casino's insurance company. In 'Organ Grinder', two women poison each other's husbands and share their inheritances; while the investigation reveals the truth of their two crimes, it fails to yield enough convincing evidence to bring them to trial, so the DA drops the charges. Sometimes, as in the end of 'Identity Crisis', the severing of justice from an episode's closure makes even Grissom wince. He knows the evidence traps the wrong brother in 'Alter Boys' but cannot turn it around, and the young man hangs himself in his jail cell.

In episodes like these, and they just sample the series, we have to realise that scientific truth, as Grissom believes in 'Chaos Theory', may bring closure in so far as it eventually solves the puzzle and reveals to him and his team what happened and who did it, but this type of closure does not automatically guarantee justice, whether understood in judicial or, as Paige Rycoff's parents display, more personal terms. To be sure, it may be reassuring to follow Grissom's example and conclude simply that truth is its own just outcome because, with the aid of science, the evidence does not lie. But returning to that exchange about interpreting evidence in 'The Execution of Catherine Willows', we ought to ponder if truth in *CSI* leaves its outcome unresolved – if, in pragmatic terms and as practised, even believed in by the forensic team, the truth of crime on *CSI* may have no outcome other than the science.

For an illustration, in the next chapter I want to look more closely at 'The Execution of Catherine Willows' and its outcome two years later in 'What's Eating Gilbert Grissom?'. Together, these two episodes dramatise the vexing relation of science's search for truth and its serving of justice, and in doing so they also widen the gap between the intellectual pleasure offered by the act of interpretation and the desire for a satisfying moral-legal order signified by the finality of an ending.

3 The Blue Paint Killer

'The Execution of Catherine Willows' opens with the temporary suspension of John Mathers's (Victor Bevine) death sentence just moments before it is to occur. One final legal appeal has successfully resulted in a state order for sophisticated DNA testing by the FBI's forensic lab of six pubic hairs found on the body of Charlene Roth, the young woman Mathers was convicted of murdering fifteen years previously (when DNA technology was too primitive to test the hairs for a positive identification). The prosecution and CSIs believe that Mathers also murdered two young women who were similarly abducted at random, tortured and raped, then slain and placed in a black trash bag just as Roth was.

This storyline, however, soon becomes the B plot when Grissom, Sara and Nick investigate the disappearance of Debbie Reston (Nikki Danielle Moore). The two plots meet midway through the episode when a body, found in a black trash bag, turns out to be hers. Evidence gathered from this latest case connects back to the prior ones when it turns out that a hair from the very first victim, Janet Kent, has been found on Reston's body. Furthermore, the timing of Reston's murder on the night when Mathers was to be executed seems hardly coincidental. The conclusion to be drawn is either that Mathers is innocent, since he was on death row and could not be responsible for the latest murder (the reason for Catherine's conversation with his attorney, who uses this new sex crime to argue for Mather's innocence), or that a copycat killer has emerged due to

Grissom and Catherine analyse the painted railings in the lab

all the publicity surrounding the execution and its temporary
suspension.

The case turns around with the discovery of how the killer
catches his victims: mixing blue paint with motor oil so that it will not
dry but stay tacky, he paints a railing in a woody area of the university
campus; when his victim gets paint on her hands and stops at a nearby
water fountain to wash them, the killer grabs her from behind. Yet, since
the criminalists themselves are only now discovering the significance of
the blue paint traces on all the murder victims, how could a copycat
killer know about it? Hence Grissom's satisfaction, in the dialogue I
quoted previously, when the new paint sample matches all of the earlier
ones except for the one taken from Roth's body. For this means that
Mathers is the copycat responsible solely for Roth's death, as the DNA
results now confirm beyond all doubt, and that the anonymous blue-
paint killer, 'playing a really twisted game' with the planting of Kent's
hair on Reston's body and his timing of her murder, committed the rest.
However, the CSIs still haven't a clue as to the serial killer's identity,
let alone enough evidence to build a case against him, as Brass and
Grissom bemoan right before the episode's final fade to blackness:

41

BRASS: He's going to kill again.

GRISSOM: Yeah. And all we've got is a partial fingerprint and an MO that may lead us in the right direction.

BRASS: You know sometimes in this job I'd rather be lucky than good. Maybe next time we'll get lucky.

GRISSOM: I don't believe in luck. My only real purpose is to be smarter than the bad guys to find the evidence that they didn't know they left behind and make sense of it all. Makes me very uncomfortable to realise that this guy may be smarter than me.

'The Execution of Catherine Willows' brings closure to the secondary story. With the DNA making for 'a slam dunk', as Catherine exclaims to Grissom, the execution goes on as scheduled, she attends it, and both the legal system and the victim's parents receive the justice they seek. Despite the subject matter highlighted by its title, the episode itself does not try to engage in more than a token debate about the death penalty. Rather, it envelopes the certainty of the secondary story with the uncertainty that leaves the primary story unsolved – the science here has no outcome but comes up empty-handed. There is evidence, traces of the killer's presence left behind at the Reston murder scene such as shards of prescription glasses, black fibres from a generic Chevy, the blue paint traces and the partial print from a trash bag, but it is all uninterpretable by the CSI team, making it appear that the Blue Paint Killer is indeed 'smarter' than Grissom and not just luckier. This primary story remains, as Grissom states, uncomfortably open-ended, the very antithesis of the secondary story's forensic 'slam dunk'.

Then, after a gap of two entire seasons, out of nowhere the Blue Paint Killer returns in 'What's Eating Gilbert Grissom?'. At first, it appears that science and some luck are playing into the CSI team's hands this time out. In the teaser, several young men chase what first looks like a giggling, squealing young woman wearing just panties and a bra; when the figure trips and falls into a pile of maggots, a close-up reveals him to be male, and we learn it is a fraternity hazing ritual that has ended up in the compost heap of the university's agricultural centre. Since there is no reason for the flesh-eating maggots to be there, Grissom is called in to investigate. A tooth is found but yields no DNA for identification of a putative body, so he has a sample extracted from a maggot, which proves that the victim was male and a student at the university. From all this evidence, it appears that this case has nothing to do with the Blue Paint Killer. However, in the pile of maggots brought back to the lab for examination, Greg finds scraps of black plastic and a piece of fingernail with blue paint, which Catherine matches to the samples taken from the unsolved trash-bag murders.

As the investigation uncovers more evidence, the conclusions Grissom and his team had drawn about the killer's MO in 'Execution' have to be revised. For the victim is now male, not female; instead of leaving the body in a trash bag to be found, the killer placed it in a wood chopper to be obliterated. Whereas in the past he painted existing railings, now the team discover one he installed himself before painting it. Furthermore, at this railing Grissom and Catherine find a black trash bag containing an inflatable porn doll with a note inside her mouth stating, 'I have her', as well as a hair from Debbie Reston's body.

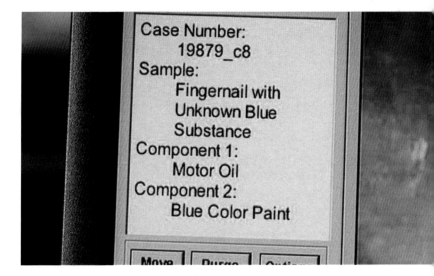

But where is this other victim? Whereas in the past the killer found refuge in his invisibility, leaving absolutely no trace of himself on a body, by planting the doll with its cryptic message, he is now addressing the investigators, toying with them directly. For that matter, in addition to the unusual double killing this time, if the Reston murder had been timed to coincide with the execution of copycat Mathers and the 'original' killer now means to celebrate the second anniversary, what accounts for his absence on that symbolic date the year before?

Although these questions remain, Grissom finds the impression of a drawing etched into the note's paper, which leads to the discovery in a black Chevy van of that other new victim alluded to in the note. From that new body and the van emerge even more gruesome insights about this 'sadistic, ritualistic, organised sociopath', as Brass describes the killer to his squad: that instead of taking photographs for souvenirs as serial killers usually do, this one draws pictures of his victims' domination from the vantage point of his van's rear-view mirror, suggesting he cannot look directly at their faces; that he rapes them with a foreign object, which is why there are no semen traces on the bodies; and that the choice of victims is intentional not random. Perhaps most important to this profile, it turns out that Mathers was not the killer's copycat but his submissive accomplice, a 'surrogate penis'. Eventually an expired parking sticker and spilled toner powder prove that the killer is an employee at the university copy centre, and this discovery leads to the commonality of the victims – all the women used the centre's services on the day of their deaths – and from this realisation to the Blue Paint Killer's identity, Kevin Greer (Taylor Nichols).

What is so striking to me throughout this gathering of evidence is how the CSI team reach their conclusions by thinking about the evidence analogically even while giving the impression that they are using science purely as a technology. The criminalists examine their findings and draw comparisons through deductive reasoning, so they are indeed 'interpreting' and not just 'hearing' the evidence. Their deductions, moreover, are accepted as facts of the case, as its irrefutable truth. Learning that the outdated parking sticker belonged to

Catherine and Warrick pore over the evidence, trying to figure out what connects the murdered women

Brass finds the Chevy van with Debbie Reston's body

Mathers, Nick reasons that he and the killer were in fact partners. Looking first at the female body in the autopsy room and then at photos of the 'pretty' dead male, Catherine notices the physical resemblance, which leads her to believe that the victims were not picked randomly but selected intentionally and, because of the likeness, that the male student was mistaken for an intended female target, that young woman later found in the van. Warrick identifies the killer's vehicle by noting the resemblance of the oblong windows in the drawing and the characteristic shape of windows on a Chevy van. The reverse lettering reflected on the car window in the drawing leads to a porn shop in a strip mall, where the team finds the van with the female victim, because Nick recognises the distinctive store signage. In the store, Grissom learns that the killer is a local amateur artist who provides his sadistic comic books for sale there in exchange for merchandise like the blow-up doll left at the latest campus crime scene. Sara's 'analysis' of the art, as she refers to it, requires little forensic testing, but rather her psychological interpretation of the artist's perverse sexual fantasies of domination and torture as revealed by the comic book's narrative content and its graphic imagery.

46

And as for the outcome of all this 'evidence'? The Blue Paint Killer remains ahead of Grissom at every turn. By the time Brass, his squad and the CSI team arrive at his house, where a paint mixer is running for their benefit, Kevin Greer is nowhere to be found. The phone rings and his answering machine picks up. Still playing with them, he leaves a message saying he is waiting for them at the police station. 'Yeah, my rule was if you made it to my house, you deserved to meet me,' Greer subsequently explains when, addressing Grissom and Brass by their first names, the three sit down to talk. 'Am I disappointing you guys?' the killer asks, since he turns out to have a rather meek and ordinary, if scruffy, demeanour. 'I mean, are you looking at me, wishing I was . . . scarier?'

During the interview, while Grissom appears to be subtly provoking the man into confessing, it slowly becomes clear that the scientist has found his match on this case. The killer fills in for Grissom

The disappointing face of Kevin Greer

the missing pieces that the evidence fails to supply, and in doing so his own eye-witness testimony, not science, legitimates the numerous conclusions the CSIs have deduced during the course of their investigation. Greer, not Grissom, is the one who makes sense of the evidence, putting it in context. Greer explains that the broken glasses in the Debbie Reston case made him realise his eyesight was a liability but the corrective Lasik surgery he undertook afterwards had complications that caused him to miss the first anniversary of Mathers's execution. The surgery, furthermore, increased his night blindness, which accounts for his killing of the college boy by mistake. That error, Greer goes on to indicate, is ultimately what 'got me caught'. In addition, Greer explains that Mathers thought he had something to prove by killing Charlene Roth on his own – 'he didn't understand that we were better together than we would ever be apart' – so his partner's conviction and execution were just outcomes in so far as 'he got caught' and 'that's the price you pay for incompetence'. But after Mathers was apprehended, Greer then 'spent fifteen years looking for a solid replacement, but you only get that lucky once in a lifetime'.

Greer then outmanoeuvres Grissom one final time.
Finding drawings in Greer's house of six, not five, victims along with
hair strands from each, Catherine realises there is still a missing body,
that of one 'Brit Moscowe'. Greer offers to lead Grissom and Brass to
this victim but asks to go to the toilet first. In the meantime, Sara notices
a calendar on the wall in Greer's house with similar drawings, and
figures out that the name is a ruse, a near anagram of 'Miss October'.
But by then Greer, alone in a toilet cubicle, has suffocated himself with a
black trash bag. Much as Greer said of his partner, having made a
mistake in killing the college boy, he too deserves to be 'caught'.

This episode, one of the creepiest and most compelling that
CSI has done so far, punctures the series's ideological view of science;
it dramatises that the team can go only so far in conceiving of science as
the transparent rendering of truth via the evidence alone. To my mind,
this is also the implication of the episode's title, 'What's Eating Gilbert
Grissom?'. For who catches whom in this case's closure? All along,
through the clues he has planted and his testimony in the episode's
fourth act, Greer has been directing the disclosure of the case's truth;
and, from the time he left the phone message – or even before then,
when he abandoned his van or, for that matter, when he left the doll with

the message, perhaps even when he placed the male body in the chopping machine – Greer and not forensic science has been moving the case toward its final outcome, the Blue Paint Killer's own gruesome execution of 'justice'. Rather than slipping up to 'leave behind' evidence that Grissom can then 'make sense of', the hope expressed at the close of 'The Execution of Catherine Willows', the killer has been orchestrating the evidence with a fully deliberated sense of purpose and intentionality that exceeds the science. The episode ends with Grissom studying what Greer was drawing throughout the interview: multiple images of Grissom reflected in the scientist's own glasses that, when folded, further reveal a smaller reflection of the Blue Paint Killer looking back at Grissom and saying, 'good bye'. He *is* smarter.

4 The *CSI* Style

Along with its concentration on forensic science, the stylised look of *CSI* immediately distinguished it from other crime shows on television. Two features of the style that stood out continue to define the series through its visual template. These are, first, the trademark 'CSI shots', which illustrate the cutting-edge forensic technology at work, display trace evidence in microscopic close-ups or probe the interior of a victim's body; and second, the highly selective use of colour separations that render a darker but also more unrealistic look than usual for TV crime shows. Although the CSI shots still get most of the attention, the colour design, manufactured through post-production digital processing, is equally crucial.[27] 'Our philosophy', former writer-director Danny Cannon explains, 'was that if the sound on your TV went out, you should still be able to know what the story's about.' To meet this requirement, he continues, the writing team had to learn 'to write visually'.[28] Already evident in the pilot and then fine-tuned in successive episodes, this style has remained consistent as a signature of the series despite changes in the production team over the years.

The style contributes greatly to how *CSI* portrays science and crime, not only in opposition to each other but also as they connect through the human body, since bodies function for the scientists as microcosmic displays of a crime scene. When creating the series, Anthony Zuiker imagined the CSI shots that travel through the body's interior or zoom in on the root of a hair follicle; in his script for the pilot, he included directions such as 'We track the bullet inside the victim'. Cannon says he took what Zuiker wrote literally, using a combination of models, periscope cameras, stop-motion cinematography, 'snap-zoom' motion acceleration, layered CGI effects and digital colour timing 'to create a point of view that we'd never before seen in television'.[29]

The CSI shot's 'point of view' has been praised and criticised for its representation of scientific authenticity. As Deborah Jermyn remarks, 'the series' success cannot be extricated from its spectacular deployment of CGI and special effects' that, notably in the CSI shot, work in concert to establish a 'privileged point of view' for rendering the impersonality and objectivity of scientific vision with authenticity.[30] For instance, 'And Then There Were None' from the second season punctuates its narrative, which opens with a casino robbery by several men in drag (and a single woman hiding in plain sight), with some half a dozen CSI shot sequences, some bolder, longer and more dramatic than others. The shots in this episode, itself inventive in its plot twists but formulaic and unproblematic in its execution, are not particularly gruesome in the manner one may expect of *CSI*, but their variety in visualising the science is nonetheless illustrative of the series as a whole.

Right after the opening credits, Catherine, investigating a separate robbery and murder at a convenience store, concludes that the bits and pieces of potato found on the floor are the residue of a 'poor man's silencer'. Like a thought balloon in a comic strip, a quick cut to a sideways view of a gun firing into a potato illustrates what she has in mind. In the meantime, one of the casino robbers is killed by one of his own during the heist. As Dr Robbins examines the body, 'shot in the back with a hollow point – close range', the anonymous camera follows the path indicated by his description of how the bullet, penetrating the flesh, 'mushroomed upon impact, maximising trauma'. Back in the convenience store, as Sara places a thin piece of silver film onto a counter in order to take shoe prints with an electrostatic machine, the camera leaves her viewpoint to move beneath the film so that it can record the prints as they appear on the underside. Nick discovers that the getaway car in the casino heist is leaking burnt transmission fluid and a series of quick edits moves further and further into the interior of the car's engine in order to show what causes the oil to fry. When potato residue is also discovered on bullets recovered from the casino heist, the episode's two cases seem connected, and another visualisation of the potato silencer in action, this time a frontal view, accompanies Catherine's explanation to Grissom. In the following scene, bullets from

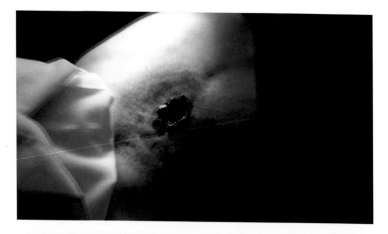

The autopsy in 'And Then There Were None'

each case are examined next to each other in a microscopic close-up shot, confirming her theory that the same gun was used in both crimes.

Along with the potato residue, white dust found on the clothing of the dead casino robber also turns out to be an important clue. Warrick finds the same dust in the car with the leaky transmission and he holds out his finger to show Nick. With a magnifying glass, Nick examines the sample. A series of edits follows but then exceeds his scrutinising gaze. The camera's position here does not simply assume Nick's viewing position but hones in on him looking, and as it gets closer to Warrick the image becomes more abstract. When the camera reaches Warrick's fingertip, however, the image sharpens and is framed by the microscope, which enables the dust to be more clearly visible in its particularities on the surface of the CSI's white glove. A snap-zoom to the microscope's view of the dust is followed by a second snap-view to an even more perfect enlargement of the crystals, which in turn effects a narrative transition in time and space to Greg identifying the composition of the sample with his magnifying lens: 'silica dust, each grain one hundred times smaller than a grain of sand'.
Finally, ballistics expert Bobby Dawson (Gerald McCullouch) examines two bullets related to the final murder in the episode, and this comparison of their stripes and grooves, shown in a microscopic close-up, prepares the way for Grissom to identify the man who murdered everyone in the casino gang – a rogue state trooper introduced early on. The silica dust on his shoes, which leads a trail to his locker where he has stashed the stolen money, clinches the arrest.

One other instance of CGI work in this episode should also be noted since, although not technically a CSI shot, it is an important cousin to it. With the known members of the casino gang all dead, the CSIs run out of suspects, so Archie Johnson (Archie Kao), the A/V tech, returns to the surveillance footage, which he digitally alters as Grissom and Sara look on. Archie removes the disguise and rebuilds the image 'based on male physiological norms' in order to show what the one unidentifiable member would look like out of drag. A close-up of Archie's computer screen displays his image manipulation: he isolates the figure from the

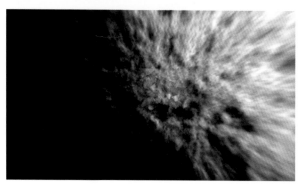

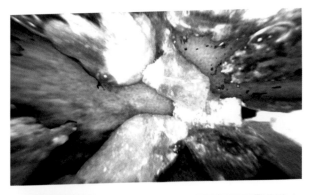

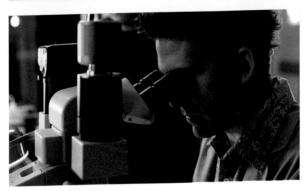

Examining the silica dust in 'And Then There Were None'

Archie manipulates the surveillance footage

background, overlays a graph upon it, removes the wig, highlights the dark glasses in green, replaces them with eyes chosen from a menu to the right of the main screen or window on the monitor, and reveals the clerk killed at the convenience store.

56

This sequence, interrupted once by a reverse shot to Archie in order to stabilise his point of view toward the monitor, relates to the other CSI shots in this episode in two ways. First, with the altered figure shown in the large window and the original image as well as the removed wig appearing in small windows to the side, the monitor displays multiple viewpoints simultaneously, creating an impersonal visual omniscience akin to that achieved by the CSI shot. Second, Archie's digital manipulation, undertaken in the interest of enhancing the evidence ('that's what I'm here for', he says proudly), replicates the process of digital manipulation by which the CSI shots are themselves achieved, a point I shall return to later on and again in the next chapter.

Zuiker himself states his inspiration for the CSI shot was the 1999 film *Three Kings*, which had a comparable interior view following bullets into a body. For an even earlier anticipation of the CSI shot, members of the creative team also cite an older film, *Fantastic Voyage*

(1966), which imagined the ability of science to miniaturise a team of doctors so that they could travel inside a body via the blood stream to perform delicate brain surgery from within.[31] These passing remarks about the shot's ancestry imply its creative value as spectacle but also obscure an equally important debt. As Jermyn points out, the CSI shot visually draws on 'the realist connotations' of a visual technology in medicine that is becoming ever more common and familiar to *CSI*'s viewers: for instance, the use of probing endoscopic cameras in conjunction with video imaging in procedures like a colonoscopy.[32] TV medical documentaries incorporating this technology, both to represent what it does and to simulate how it can view the body's interior, further prepared the way for the CSI shot.

With this medical context as a point of reference, the CSI shot legitimates a pair of related assumptions, dominant in our culture, about the truthfulness of science through visuality: that, in the words of Marita Sturken and Lisa Cartwright, 'scientific truths are understood as providing the capacity to see "truths" that are not available to the human eye' and, correspondingly, that 'images are seen as "scientific" when they are held to present accurate, self-evident proof of certain facts'.[33] Visualising the viewpoint of science, with the CSIs using machines to see what the eye alone cannot, the series's style appears to reinforce the neutrality and hence authenticity of what Martha Gever calls 'a world where electronic mastery provides solutions to all mysteries, full disclosure of all secrets, discovery of all truths. Even the tiniest, mundane residues of human life can incriminate.'[34]

As a result, from the inserted CSI shots and chilly blue colours of the lab area to the grainy monochromatic flashbacks that progressively sort through subjective accounts of a crime, the style reinforces what the investigative narratives dramatise, namely, the unimpeachable value of scientific vision. The science behind the crime lab's investigation of cases requires the dismantling and probing of corpses, turning the human body into an object of close scrutiny and, through technology, transforming its hidden interior into a visible surface. But the objectification of the body by science, epitomised by those CSI shots that visualise autopsy findings, implies a striking parallel with the objectification of the body in consumer culture, too.

The second season finale, 'The Hunger Artist', implicitly juxtaposes forensic science's impersonal probing of bodies, whether through the medical examiner's scalpel or the lab's DNA testing, with the fashion industry's exploitation of women's bodies. The body of model Ashleigh James (Tricia Helfer), formerly the source of her fame and fortune, evinces her victimisation by an industry that, as her agent unabashedly states to Catherine, treats women like various cuts of meat in a butcher shop. At first, the CSIs presume that the multiple wounds on the dead woman's face resulted from torture or someone's rage, but it turns out they were self-inflicted. Suffering from both bulimia and anorexia (with Dr Robbins's explanation illustrated by CSI shots), Ashleigh had, after being dropped by her agent, repeatedly gouged out what she perceived as imperfections in her face, causing her own body to become septic, the cause of her death. Additionally, once Sara finally decodes the symbolic notations in Ashleigh's day planner, more disturbing manifestations of the model's BDD or Body Dysmorphic Disorder come to light: in an effort to maintain her body's symmetry, all the while binging on junk food and purging it afterwards, Ashleigh recorded in shorthand every quarter gram eaten and every quarter gram eliminated as bodily waste, thereby making certain that what was taken in was cancelled out by what was expelled, usually with the aid of enemas. 'Control and perfection,' Sara comments, '. . . that's what her code was all about.' Upon hearing this explanation, Grissom observes: 'And so, she was, uh, operating like a scientist, seeking a perfect formula to take her pain away.'

Although it is barely stated by 'The Hunger Artist', the discomforting comparability of Ashleigh's 'science', relying on its own binary notations of pluses and minuses, and the CSIs' cannot be easily ignored. There is an obvious parallel between the body's status as an object of voyeuristic appeal both in fashion and on television, to which I shall return in the next chapter. More pertinent to my point about the

Sara decodes Ashleigh James's shorthand for the rest of the CSI team

rendering of scientific vision as truthfulness, once deciphered by Sara, Ashleigh's coded day planner makes the body's interior more legible.

    Stylistically as well as narratively, and despite red herrings and mistaken initial conclusions, the body of a victim is a recurring source of fascination as well as information on *CSI*. The body is a malleable surface, as made evident by its bruising, disfigurement or defilement, first during a crime and then during an autopsy. Furthermore, and not unlike the coded notations in Ashleigh's day planner, science shows how the body is more than the surface visible to the naked eye. The body has volume and depth, with its interior comprising additional layers of malleable and legible materiality – organs extracted, weighed and measured at an autopsy; the DNA in blood, saliva or semen sampled, run through computer programs and translated into a coloured spreadsheet. Particularly as rendered by the visual style of *CSI*, science's ability to visualise the body's interiority is in its way also a form of 'control and perfection'.

    Even more provocatively, the considerable investment in the visual as the basis of scientific truth, the premise behind the CSI shot and the series's 'look' as a whole, is mired in a fundamental paradox about visuality, which *CSI* knowingly depends upon and exploits in numerous ways, beginning with its style. After all, visuality can never really be purely neutral, a point repeatedly made by scholars like Gever who critique *CSI* for promoting, especially in an era of Photoshop image manipulation, the 'magical property of photography: a visualization of technology associated with the idea of unmediated truth'.[35]

However, *CSI* does not treat visuality so naively. While the series associates the omnipresent microscope and camera, both crucial tools of the CSIs in their investigations, with the objectivity of impersonal (the camera) and distanced (the microscope) scientific vision, this vision is itself rendered through a style that forsakes realism. The CSI shots are not only 'excessive', as Elke Weissman and Karen Boyle note, 'adding little to our knowledge or intellectual understanding of the crime',[36] but they are also so elaborately and self-consciously stylised that they challenge the realist connotations of medical imaging even as they model themselves upon it. With the stylisation always visible to the TV viewer as a deliberately crafted look, as a mode of representation mediating what occurs in the narrative, the signature CSI look quite literally determines our view of what the science purportedly sees as 'accurate, self-evident proof'.

A moment in 'I Like to Watch' from season six self-reflexively calls attention to the paradox of visuality on *CSI*. Nick tells David Hodges (Wallace Langham), who tests for trace evidence, that Grissom wants him to compare adhesives on two pieces of duct tape. Aware of the reality-show crew wandering around the lab with their video equipment, the always self-important Hodges cheerfully says, 'That'll take a laser ablation test. That's good.' When Nick asks, 'Why's that good?' Hodges replies, 'Well, laser ablation is both visual and dramatic.' Laughing, Nick tells him to relax: 'the show's only an hour long. Laser ablation takes, like, six.' But well aware of how TV can manipulate raw footage through editing, Hodges reminds Nick: 'Yeah, but when they cut it together, it'll take only thirty seconds.' Nick leaves.

'Laser ablation is both visual and dramatic'

Glancing around to see if the reality show's crew is there to record his work, Hodges removes the pieces of tape from the evidence bag, places a cutting in the laser ablation machine and begins the testing process. A thirty-second CSI shot takes the camera inside the machine to show the lasers burning a diamond-shaped pattern into the piece of tape, after which the fine, ashy residue is sucked into a vacuum tube.

'I Like to Watch' brings reality TV into the fictional world of CSI, showing how the voyeuristic TV crew intrudes upon, interrupts and seeks to sensationalise the work of forensic investigation. This sequence, like other self-reflexive moments in the episode, no doubt means to address criticism of CSI's own lack of fidelity to realism; here, the gentle self-parody acknowledges that the series makes no pretence of occurring in 'real' time. But in aiming its joke at that criticism, this sequence has to expose the disarming conjunction of scientific authenticity and televisual spectacle signified by the CSI shot. On one hand, the sequence confirms the shot's legitimacy as a source of seeing what the naked eye cannot see, which is how CSI represents the truthfulness of scientific vision. In contrast with the video equipment of the absent reality-show crew, the series's own camera can zoom inside the laser ablation machine; this endoscopic camera is, by association, treated as if it were another impartial instrument of science. On the other hand, the dialogue recognises that the CSI shot is itself a product of technological manipulation, beginning with the special-effect camerawork and extending to the editing, as we are made fully aware that the shot lasts half a minute while the machine itself needs several hours in 'real time'. The stylised rendition of the machine's vision thus gives the shot its added aesthetic value as a 'visual and dramatic' image. The sequence momentarily demystifies the CSI shot because it confirms that the 'look' of science as an instrument of vision and the 'look' of the series in representing that vision are never in perfect alignment. A comparable dissonance between the eye of science and the eye of television resonates as strongly, if not as explicitly, in every episode of CSI because of its stylised use of colour.

While updated each year, the main credits sequence immediately tells us to pay close attention to the special uses of colour separations as the series's principal means of visualising science and crime. In the template used until season six (at which point the sequence was considerably jazzed up), images rendered in full naturalistic colour alternate with many more that are dominated by luminous greens or blues. Green reflects the glow of a computer screen, derives from the concentrated artificial lighting in the lab area and saturates a CGI animated close-up of trace evidence as it breaks down into its molecular structure. Blue takes over night-time and darkly lit interior scenes, enveloping actors in shadows or blocking out their silhouetted figures. With red entirely drained out of most shots, the compensatory over-saturation of blue and green, either singly or in combination, results in a video image that looks as if the red component cable has become detached from the TV. Even the white letters spelling out CSI: Crime Scene Investigation appear against a blue and green background. The full-colour shots, some of which are used to identify the regular cast by name, still have a preponderance of blue or green in them, since red appears mainly to add chromatic texture to lips, skin and hair. Red appears with more vibrancy, competing with blue and green, in the

The CSI title card

stock footage of Las Vegas's skyline, where all three primary colours burst against the night in the electronic signage of the casino-hotels. The few times that red dominates a quickly passing shot – an apple exploding or a blood drop falling against a bluish-white surface – this colour seems like a subliminal exclamation mark. Provisionally, then, the credits sequence establishes visual associations linking green with the computer technology of the lab, blue with the shadowy nocturnal world the team inhabits during the graveyard shift and red with the violent crimes they investigate.

63

  In an essay on the visual style of *CSI* and its spin-offs, Janine Hiddlestone follows these associations when comparing the individualised colour schemes of the three shows. She notes,

> Each has a thematic color and style that makes it almost instantly recognizable even without the regular characters. These themes reflected not only the geographic space, but also the characters, the crimes, the techniques, the storylines, and the subjective location of the show.

In the original *CSI*, Hiddlestone goes on to observe, the signature colour is fluorescent green in comparison with hot yellow for the sun-drenched Miami setting and smoky blue for the smoggy New York location:

> Green hues in Las Vegas are the color of fluorescence and the color of money: two essential aspects of Vegas. But it goes deeper than those obvious markers. For the crime scene investigators, the city is not a holiday destination, or a place of glamour and frivolity; their Vegas is one of darkness, seedy violence, and a soul-destroying greed. And it is also their home. For them, what happens in Vegas *really does stay* in Vegas. It is no coincidence that the show focuses on the night shift, as that is when it is all happening in Las Vegas, at least to outward appearances. In the windowless casinos it is perpetual night, a world lit only by fluorescence and muted colors, a visual situation repeated in the most utilized sets of the show: the lab. This creates a dualism that is constantly in opposition – it conveys a sense of both claustrophobia and safety.

'The only space the green cannot infect is the morgue,' she concludes, 'which is always bathed in shades of blue; it is a place of peace and sadness, beyond the horror and suffering of the living world.'[37]

Generally speaking, this scheme holds up, although it is important to add that colour does not consistently bear the valences that Hiddlestone describes; nor did green remain the identifiable *CSI* colour except on the CBS website and the DVD packaging in the USA. As in the credits sequence, blue was used during the first two seasons for discrete lighting effects and nocturnal exterior scenes, while green dominated scenes occurring in the lab areas and interview room, suggesting the parallel with the casinos Hiddlestone notices. But toward the end of season two, the white walls of the entire lab set (the evidence room, trace, DNA, fingerprints, ballistics, Grissom's office, even the garage) were repainted what production designer Richard Berg calls 'the *CSI* colour, grey-blue', a change made so that the actors would stand out better spatially when filmed.[38] Then, from the third season onward, blue progressively became the main *CSI* colour in the lab and interview room, present in the set design, lighting, lens filters or gels, even costuming (blue jumpsuits, blue suits, blue shirts or blouses). In these scenes, whenever green appears, whether in its own right or with a yellowish glimmer, this colour backlights actors otherwise awash in blue, imparts volume to the density of the blue space behind them, fills in the shadows on their bluish faces or adds reflections on glass cabinets in the rear of the lab's blue-grey set. If red shows up in a lab scene, apart from adding skin tone, the colour is placed there for the purpose of an eye-catching visual composition. Red is usually confined to the margins of the screen, shining on a small area of the blue background to reflect a secondary and weaker light source, even if just an exit sign; or it is isolated as the singular colour of an object illuminated by the radiance of a pale blue light positioned beneath or over the glass evidence table. (It's worth noting, too, that such attention to a shot's visual composition through colour forces greater recognition on the viewer's part that what he or she is doing is looking, much as the CSIs are doing.)

Once identified with the colour blue, the lab environment became more closely allied with the chilly, antiseptic feel originally evident only in the medical examiner's autopsy room, which was blue from the start. As this happened, the colour separations in the style's palette more markedly detached the lab and its inhabitants from the greenish tint of casino or nightclub scenes and their connotations of greed and chance, from the neon red of crime scenes, which are particularly of this hue when they have a sexual basis or are extremely bloody, and from the sandy yellow of daylight scenes shot in Las Vegas's many tract housing developments and gated communities or the outlying desert. Intensifying the lab's cloistered atmosphere, blue now more fully brings out the advantage and possibly also the cost of the 'safer' – in so far as it is more contemplative, disinterested, tranquil, but also cool and unemotional – space of science as personified by the intellectualism and isolation of Grissom and his team.

As indicated a moment ago, however, we should not try to make colour bear too heavy a burden, because the series's design does not faithfully adhere to a symbolic system mapping out the terrain of its world. Lab scenes are mainly dressed, lit and filtered in blue, but

'The *CSI* colour'

sometimes they are rendered more naturalistically with a fuller colour spectrum, just as night scenes outside the lab or in dark interiors may take blue as their dominant colour. Moreover, at times the series's use of colour follows some established conventions of continuity editing borrowed from film. The blue colour within a lab scene may be varied so that it follows the rhythm of shot/reverse-shot perspective: if Grissom's

face is shaded in blue, say, the person speaking with him may be noticeably backlit with a greenish or reddish glow from another light source.

An episode's narrative progression may at times also motivate the colouring of a particular scene regardless of where it is set. In the same way that the establishing shots of Las Vegas buildings in full colour mark an obvious shift to a new locale, a change in the colour palette visually signals a corresponding transition in the plot as it travels to another space (from the lab out into the field), time (from the present to the past via flashback reconstructions of a crime) or perspective (from Dr Robbins performing an autopsy to a CSI shot displaying what he describes), or as it segues between primary and secondary cases.

Additionally, when the nearly exclusive use of blue, green or red in a scene stays within the dark-to-light range of that single colour tone, the effect serves the purpose of visual intrigue more than it demarcates a symbolic topography: space is obscured by shadows, marked by contrasting planes of light and dark, or illuminated so that the human figure is silhouetted by a whitish halo. The monochromatic design of such scenes intentionally evokes how classic film noir manipulated black-and-white cinematography in order to imply claustrophobia, alienation, menace and secrets.

It is probably safest to conclude simply that the *CSI* style carefully deploys colour in order to compel viewer attention.

A single colour creates a film noir-like effect for purposes of visual intrigue

The absence or presence of a primary colour in any one scene makes the stylised imagery stand out as part of an overall design conveying some sort of meaning or intent in so far as the style announces, 'You are watching *CSI*'. But, following Hiddlestone, we can push this thought a bit further: because the colour separation is particularly distinctive due to its repetition, the style solicits viewer interest precisely by virtue of its ability to supply a visual trigger, organising associations that enable subtler appreciation of the tonal and hence thematic differences between the lab and the outside world, between science and crime. In doing so, however, the style also self-consciously asserts that, as Silke Panse points out, '*CSI* is about the procedures of processing, with respect not only to the logistics of crime, but also to the processed images of the series itself'.[39] Both the CSI shots and the stylised colour design reveal the extent to which two opposing frameworks for looking, science and TV, occupy a common ground in digital imaging. Stylistically, *CSI* is most visually compelling, I think, when it calls explicit attention to the intriguing paradox that results from the way it represents science as something to be looked *at* as well as a viewpoint to be looked through.

5 Looking at Science

The intent to craft a distinctive *CSI* style so that episodes would tell the story 'visually as much as it was going to be told in words' originated with producer Jerry Bruckheimer.[40] With a goal of sustaining his trademark of compelling – which is also to say long, loud and explosive – visual spectacle in his blockbuster action films while adapting it to the quieter, less action-driven narrative premise of *CSI*, Bruckheimer's plan was to 'apply feature-quality production values to primetime TV and produce mini-movies each week'.[41] 'It was very important to him', executive producer Carol Mendelsohn remembered on the occasion of the franchise's 300th episode, 'that when viewers flipped the channels and saw *CSI*, they'd say, "That's a Bruckheimer show." '[42]

Danny Cannon kept that instruction in mind when filming the pilot in 2000. 'I approached the pilot as a feature film, with feature film coverage, the way we went about designing it, casting it, the attention to detail, the attention to post-production.'[43] From watching the series, we know that the self-identifying slogan of *CSI* is 'the evidence never lies'. But as far the series's production team is concerned, visual effects supervisor Andrew Orloff still declares in one of the season six DVD supplements, 'the mantra of *CSI* is the feature for television'.[44] As discussed in the previous chapter, the *CSI* style does regularly copy filmic qualities, both old (high contrasts and murky shadows in the tradition of film noir) and new (colour filtering and separations, and CGI effects), achieving the standard of 'quality' feature film-making that the production team invoke through their interviews and commentaries.

That said, the goal of making every episode of *CSI* a 'mini-movie' is a somewhat lofty ambition, at least when considering the speed with which series television needs to be produced. For all the care and artistry that go into it, each episode of *CSI* has an eight-day shooting schedule; while one director, such as Cannon, films a script with the actors, another director, such as Richard J. Lewis, supervises post-production of the episode he has previously shot the week or so before, and still another director, such as Kenneth Fink, works with the set, make-up, props, sound, special effects and casting departments to prepare for his direction of the next episode to be filmed. Meanwhile, the writing team is coming up with ideas for new episodes, researching them and finishing scripts so that they are ready to go to show runner Carol Mendelsohn for the final (and ordinarily uncredited) polish. Despite the lead time with which production of *CSI* starts up again each year during the summer, the directors mention on their DVD commentary tracks that by mid-season they often find themselves delivering a finished product to CBS right before it is scheduled to air.[45]

Given Bruckheimer's track record as a producer of big blockbuster movies, moreover, his equating the 'quality' of a feature film with its production values in order to highlight how *CSI* is instantly recognisable as 'a Bruckheimer show' reflects today's commercial film aesthetic, which tends to structure big-budget features kinetically as if they were roller-coaster rides. Critics have stressed how, with its fast-paced editing, arresting colour design, and aestheticised depiction of microscopic particles and pulsating bodily organs, *CSI* offers TV viewers a comparable pleasure. For instance, Weissman and Boyle observe how, due to their speed and their gore, the CSI shots have the effect on viewers of correlating 'cerebral knowledge about the body' with 'bodily experience of this knowledge'.[46] Inciting an emotional, even physical response to what science sees, these shots – such as the gun firing through the potato in 'And Then There Were None', or the bullet ripping through flesh at close range, or the gears burning transmission oil or the snap-zoom magnification of the silica dust – work upon viewers through rapid editing in much the same way that explosions, car chases and choreographed hand-to-hand combat engage spectators of an action film; the shot's kinetic affect, according to this line of thought, is what makes the imagery so pleasurable and that pleasure seem so film-like.

However, *CSI* is not cinema; shots are framed for the letterbox ratio of high-definition television and the final cut of each episode is transferred from Super 35 film to HD video prior to airing.[47] An episode is typically photographed in a relatively even range of colour, often aiming for a warmish cast to preserve skin tones. Then, in order to achieve the distinctive '*CSI* look', the footage is digitally altered in post-production. On some of the early episodes, Roy Wagner, the series's first director of photography, and Gareth Cooke, who supervises post-production for the series at Encore Hollywood, used a software program that can approximate the specialised 'bleach bypass' technique of film processing. That method omits the bleaching stage that would otherwise remove silver grains from the emulsion; the goal is to retain both a layer of colour and a layer of black and white, superimposing one over the other to give the image a more desaturated and connotatively 'edgy' look. Simulating this process on a computer rather than imposing it on the master negative in a film lab, Wagner and Cooke manipulated the contrasts, brightness and chromatic texture of what was shot; they adjusted lights and shadows, and subtracted some colour values from the source footage, all in order to achieve the certain ambience of a scene intended by the script and prepared for by the way it was lit for filming.[48]

Even though the *CSI* production team follows Bruckheimer's lead in describing the show's visual quality as 'filmic', we therefore ought not to ignore what is, at least by the end of the process, a digitally manufactured *video* style. Repeatedly insisting on a 'quality' feature-film standard may reflect a desire on the part of the production team to make *CSI* more than just another crime show, but it also reveals how, when the series began in 2000, the thinking behind its crafted look at least implicitly anticipated the transformation of both the TV medium and its viewers as they moved together into the high-definition era of the new century. 'If you haven't seen *CSI* in high definition,' announced an unnamed CBS executive at the annual Las Vegas consumer electronics trade show in 2006, '. . . you haven't seen *CSI*.' After watching a demonstration on a fifty-foot HD set, Jack Tirak, the media blogger reporting this remark, enthusiastically agreed. 'The detail of the evidence in extreme close-ups', he reported, 'is like nothing you have ever seen.'[49]

If the motivation for what became the distinctive *CSI* style was to prompt viewer recognition of 'a Bruckheimer show' when switching channels, the corollary purpose was surely to get viewers not only to stop at the CBS station but then to watch with rapt attention. With its heavy reliance on blues and greens and strategic use of reds, the *CSI* style foregrounds the three primary colours of human vision – and of video. This is why, as Tirak observed, *CSI* looks most striking on a high-definition television that makes full use of the chromatic separation of a video signal into three channels, either via component or HDMI cables.[50] Likewise, an episode's stylised colour is more vivid even on standard DVD, which also digitally encodes that separation, than on a standard analogue cable feed. Moreover, since the style's separation of colour is achieved through digital manipulation when, as happens in every episode of *CSI*, the luminosity of blue, green or red in a scene or CSI shot makes the colour 'pop' and seem 'electric' because of its intensity and vibrancy, these widely used terms for figuratively describing colour in a state of unnatural brightness ought to be taken literally too, in so far as the style brings out how the colours on the TV screen are indeed an electronic phenomenon.

One episode that carries its narrative through colour and in so doing explicitly pushes the act of looking into the foreground is 'After the Show' from season four. This is an unusual episode in two respects. First, in a reversal of the usual pattern of the series, when it opens the CSIs have a suspect who appears guilty but they lack evidence that a major crime has been committed. Second, and not unrelated to this quandary in the narrative, colour separations conspicuously organise the episode from beginning to end, forcing us as *CSI*'s viewers to think

73

more intently about the stylisation of what we see and to consider what it achieves.

'After the Show' opens with the standard colour shot of Las Vegas: a casino-hotel with an outdoor video advertisement of its showgirl revue. Over the shot, a female voice talks about her lifelong ambition to be a showgirl. As the voice continues, an edit joins the speech to a face, and a young woman can be seen speaking in a grainy coloured video. A blue hand touches her image, followed by the revelation that the hand belongs to a male stroking a large-screen TV while phoning 911. His body radiates, as if blue light from the television were passing right through him; but the intensity of this single colour also flattens his body so that he seems like an electronic cut-out placed over the video image, which, because of its comparatively fuller, if washed-out, colours, seems to exist in a more real three-dimensional space. With an edit to a close-up, the man's face then appears in profile, his skin still emitting blue light. He places a gun to his mouth and mutters, 'I never meant to hurt her.'

After a shot of this man on his hands and knees, a dissolve over his prostrate body reveals the CSIs, Brass and a SWAT team gathering outside the house, followed by a cut to a more distanced view of the night-time exterior. The implied violence occurring inside the house now

travels outside. The man has not pulled the trigger; and as a noisy crowd of TV reporters and neighbourhood bystanders gather to watch, Brass and his men wrestle him down, then place him under arrest.

Visually adding to the commotion, the full colour of the exterior setting is saturated in dark blue except for red lights flashing atop police cars, the vehicles' white headlights and a helicopter's searchlight, all of which illuminate the emerald green lawn. The lawn's colour is unnaturally green: after all, it is night and Vegas is an arid climate, but what is more, the lawn glows with an excessive brightness that almost makes it look as if the green tint level is turned up too high on the TV. The lawn shines so intensely against the night that, despite the ostensible presence of the police cars' headlights and the helicopter overhead, the grass itself appears to be the main source of illumination. From the CSIs' conversation we learn that the young woman in the video is a missing person probably killed by the man who keeps saying he never meant to hurt her; as they supply this exposition, their figures in the dark-blue setting of the scene are backlit by the lawn's green glow.

Following the opening credits and a fleeting return to the exterior, Catherine and Sara walk through the empty house. The TV is still on, showing a live news report of what is happening outside.

77

The interior of the living room is overwhelmed by blue shadows that somehow do not reach the green carpeting, which also glows, its luminescence matching that of the lawn outside. Catherine's head and shoulders are sculpted by blue shadows but her hair reflects the greenish-yellow of the carpet. As the two women go through the dark room, they pick up newspapers and magazines from piles strewn around the floor and on the furniture. Inserted close-ups display in full colour what they examine by way of a flashlight in the darkened blue room, revealing that the woman we saw on video is Julie Waters (Jaime Ray Newman), a wannabe showgirl. As the two investigators make their way into another room, a shot in full colour, this time of the yellowish kitchen where another TV is on, gives the viewer a clearer sense of the house's spatial layout, but that sense of perspective disappears when successive shots again drench the scene in blue shadows.

Then, with a cut that takes Catherine and Sara into an adjoining photography studio, they are suddenly awash in red light, and this unexpected intrusion of the colour, I think, means to take the audience by surprise. The scene itself, though, turns out to be benign – the investigators find displayed there more photos of Julie Waters and a business card identifying the suspect as Howard Delhomme (Martin Donovan), photographer – and the red glow, which recedes as more lights are switched on, has a logical source in the studio. This scene consequently has no narrative cause for its brief jolting effect only a stylistic one. The momentary shift to red hints at, but without confirming, what the CSIs and the audience must be thinking: that Julie Waters is a victim, that the crime is her murder and that its violence is of a sexual nature.

The exaggerated colour separations set up during this long opening sequence remain in place as the guiding principle of visual organisation for the remainder of 'After the Show'. The lab and interview room, the recurring locale once the team leaves Delhomme's house, are their expected shades of blue. In some of these scenes, blue light floods over the actors; at other times it separates them from the background. The actors themselves wear blue for the most part, or a

black that could be dark navy. When, accompanied by Delhomme, the CSI team and the police travel to the desert to look for Julie Waters's body, the darkening and lightening of the clear blue sky, sped up by jump-cut editing, indicate the passage of time as the search goes into the night and comes up empty-handed early the next morning. Later on, once the team figures out where Delhomme buried Waters in the desert, Nick and Greg carefully dig up her body in order to preserve trace evidence, and this discovery scene is tinted pale blue, just like when Dr Robbins later examines her corpse. By contrast, Delhomme wears a red prison jumpsuit that stands out against the greyish blue surrounding him in the interview room and the blue sky of the desert nightscape. With the audience well primed by that earlier scene in his home studio, the presence of red alongside the blue seems menacing because it fights with, but is contained by, the more dominant colour. Every time Delhomme subsequently appears in the episode, the singular colour of his jumpsuit incites an expectation that he will be violent. That finally happens in the climax. Delhomme explodes in rage and, though shackled to his chair, strikes out at Catherine, who has been leading this investigation, when she confronts him with the evidence proving his guilt.

80

Early in 'After the Show', Catherine tells Sara: 'We found this guy in pieces and he's been putting himself together ever since.' The extreme blueness of the opening scenes, their composition jarringly intersected by the green lawn and carpeting, visualises Delhomme's irrational state, which the CSIs must then probe but also counteract in order to find out what has happened. For this reason, the dominance of blue in the opening may seem at odds with how this colour ordinarily functions on *CSI* to represent the lab in opposition to a crime scene. The unnatural blue and green colouring of the opening scenes creates an unsettling landscape that registers Delhomme's disorientation but at the same time, because of the colours' past associations with the lab as a safe space of rational, impartial vision, it visually brings Delhomme's state of mind into dangerously close proximity to the CSIs, incorporating them into the irrational, distorted vision they are meant to oppose.

True, Delhomme is the antithesis of someone like Catherine or Grissom, and his agitation initially contrasts with their poise when they collect and evaluate evidence. Furthermore, Delhomme's association with the colour red once he is taken into police custody and starts 'putting himself together' undermines his later declaration of innocence; simultaneously, the association underscores his predatory sexual attraction to Catherine. Yet just as Delhomme's house turns out not to have been a crime scene, nothing is quite what it seems. Catherine proves that his disorientation at the start was itself an act, the manufacturing of an alibi; his feigned suicide attempt intended to supply a logical explanation of why his DNA would eventually be found on the gun used to violate Waters before killing her. Delhomme's growing self-control, at once covering up and, we can infer from the rage and misogyny it represses, motivating his sexual crime, is not entirely unlike the disciplined thinking required by science after all. While no Blue Paint Killer, Delhomme is much more in command of events than his irrational demeanour evinces to the CSIs: for all the tumult he may (or may not) be experiencing, at least until he fully loses his self-control with Catherine in the final act, he has been thinking ahead at every step.

81

Because Catherine does not learn until quite late in the episode that Delhomme had an ulterior motive in staging his suicide attempt while phoning for emergency assistance, in retrospect the extremely stylised opening of 'After the Show' may seem wilfully misleading – just a snare to grab the viewer – but to me it also seems more meaningful than that. The colour separations registering Delhomme's disorientation contaminate what ought to be the contrasting world of science, as the blueness of both his house and the lab makes troublingly clear. Visually, the difference between the two spaces amounts to that eerie green glow of both the interior and exterior of his house; the chromatic parallelism of Delhomme's house and the lab correlates with how he oscillates between self-control and violence, while implying as well that the difference between the lab and the outside world may not be science but crime.

The script then puts the visual connection between criminal and scientist in terms of character psychology. Delhomme is sexually drawn to Catherine because of her showgirl bearing, and he gets off on manipulating the investigation to keep her in his presence. Catherine decides to make use of that attraction, however unpleasant. 'I saw the look in Howard's eye,' she tells Sara. 'I used to make my living off that look. He wanted me. We needed him. I decided to exploit that situation. And as angry as that made you, when you're in my shoes, you'll do the same thing.' In accounting for her ability to recognise 'that sleazy, predatory look', Catherine's past likewise explains why she takes over the investigation despite Nick and Sara's objections (they were first on the scene of Waters's disappearance and each assumes solving this high-profile case will result in a promotion). Not only does she understand the psychology of this type of criminal, but Catherine's prior career as an exotic dancer affords a logical reason as to why crime and science should visually come into such close contact with each other in this episode. Catherine has lived the difference between Delhomme's world and the scientist's, so she guarantees, by keeping watch for, their separation.

Given the dominance of blue throughout this episode, moreover, every cut to a shot in full colour implies a corresponding

sense of growing visual clarity, slowly recording the CSIs'
understanding of what happened to Julie Waters in the desert. As the
case unfolds, the editing more regularly alternates between blue and
full colour scenes; at the same time Catherine, too, is lit to reflect a
fuller colour spectrum even when working in the blue lab or evidence
room. Significantly, aside from the occasional stock footage of Vegas
and those shots of Catherine, full colour tends to return mainly in four
types of image: long shots of the outlying desert in daylight, the place
where Julie Waters was violated, murdered and buried by Delhomme;
reverse shots indicating what a team member or lab tech is examining
(slides of her apartment or of her modelling for Delhomme, a hot pink
post-it in her day planner, a map of the desert area on a computer
screen, Delhomme's receipts from a convenience store and an
expensive car rental agency); blurry flashbacks (with significant use of
blue in Waters's shirt) as one of the CSIs theorise what happened; and
video. As in the opening, at several points various lab technicians
watch continuing news reports of the crime on a TV in the lab, its
grainy colour screen set apart from the blue surroundings. In addition,
excerpts from Waters's audition tape for a reality TV series, 'Real
Vegas Showgirls', which began the episode, also closes it, and the CSIs
watch this colour video during their investigation in order to study the
victim.

     The presence of video footage throughout the episode helps to
include *CSI*'s viewers in the wider cultural context of Delhomme's
criminality. His professional objectification of women, which the
episode connects with his misogynistic rage and predatory sexuality, is
not an uncommon occurrence on *CSI* because of the Las Vegas locale,
and references to Catherine's past, both through Delhomme's interest in
her as a showgirl and her empathetic understanding of Waters, remind
us of that fact. The post-it in the victim's day planner, shown in colour
close-up, lists two appointments scheduled on the day of her death – the
photo shoot with Delhomme and a dinner meeting afterwards with
producers of the reality TV show – which, much as the earlier 'Hunger
Artist' does, further link the particularities of this crime and its setting in

a culture of popular entertainment thriving on exploited women and
voyeuristic men. The video footage running throughout the episode then
visualises that context to make the point inescapable. 'Julie Waters
became Las Vegas's postmortem sweetheart,' Grissom comments in the
episode's conclusion, referring to how the TV coverage has given this
case its high-profile importance. 'The media as moral conscience,' he
adds ironically. 'She couldn't get away from him and he couldn't get
away from her,' Catherine replies with equal irony, recalling for us how

'The media as moral conscience,' Grissom comments to Catherine about the TV coverage of Julie Waters's disappearance and murder

the episode opens: not only with the televisions in Delhomme's house displaying Waters's face but with her appearance on every channel he switches to while making his incoherent confession in the 911 phone call.

Delhomme cannot get away from Waters because, in publicising her disappearance and murder, the media exploits her image for commercial reasons much as photographers and entertainment producers have previously done. On her part, Waters cannot get away from the likes of Delhomme even before he takes her out to the desert, because of her ambition to be a showgirl. When Sara disapproves of the expensive stockings Waters wore, Catherine explains it was a 'capital investment. Our victim hadn't made it to the show yet. Her life was all about after the show.' The audition tape presumes to lay bare a more private, less exhibitionistic view of Waters, in so far as her monologue is presumably unrehearsed and candid, but it also confirms her own role as a willing if innocent victim of a culture that has taught her that beauty, not intelligence, is her only asset, as Catherine also tries to help Sara to understand. But while 'After the Show' offers this critique of Las Vegas as a culture of voyeurism, the inserted video footage from Waters's audition tape and the news coverage incorporating it supply one of the main ways this episode itself visualises the young woman's story.

Hence the tone of Grissom and Catherine's summation in the episode's conclusion is double-edged, referring to a culture saturated in ethically dubious media imagery and to the complicity in that culture of *CSI* itself as a TV crime show with its own voyeuristic appeal. 'The construction of the television image within the series is seductive,' Karen Lury comments, using language that echoes the voyeur–exhibitionist relation of Delhomme and Waters, 'and while it strives for legitimacy by suggesting that the image is to be read as evidence, it also betrays a disturbing fascination with what it means to look at and be fascinated by images in this way.' Noting, for instance, how the obvious post-production digital manipulation of the show's style 'uncannily replicates the manipulation of the visual evidence by the characters', Lury concludes that, far from going unnoticed, 'the tension between the power of the image and a power over the image is therefore the continual tease of the programme'.[51]

Lury does not mention 'After the Show', but this episode certainly brings out the series's fascination with looking, with simultaneously viewing the image as an objectification of truthfulness and as an object that is easily manipulated – the two senses in which evidence is 'processed' on *CSI*. Perhaps because CSI shots are themselves, as Gever asserts, 'feats of micro-voyeurism'[52] and would therefore bring this tension too close to the episode's critical stance toward the media's exploitation of Waters, 'After the Show' has relatively few such shots, and those there are do not stand out in the vivid, let alone stomach-churning, manner of some other episodes.

More important, 'After the Show' makes an effort to resolve the tension inherent in *CSI*'s fascination with looking at and through science. The increasing authority of Catherine's viewpoint through the course of the investigation helps to distance her way of looking at Waters's body in photographs and on the tape from Delhomme's misogynistic gaze. One scene is constructed so that her detachment is not only explicit but gendered. In another pre-planned stab at an alibi, Delhomme digitally alters a series of photographs to make it seem that Waters posed nude for him and therefore agreed to do anything he asked of her. Comparing the nude in the photographs with digitalised shots of Waters's naked body from the autopsy, Catherine reveals that the female in Delhomme's doctored photos was not the victim.

This scene contrasts the perverse eroticism of the male voyeuristic gaze and the detached look of the female scientist, and to do it carefully distinguishes between the digitally 'cooked' and the digitally 'raw', between forged/aesthetic and truthful/scientific imagery. Before she begins to work, Catherine orders Nick, Archie and Sara to leave so she can study the photos in private. 'Look,' Catherine tells an angry Sara afterwards, 'the entire lab didn't need to see pictures of Julie's vagina plastered all over the screen.' Despite assurance in the dialogue that the photos have scientific and not prurient value, however, the camera filming the scene itself remains with Catherine after she clears the room, reminding us of *CSI*'s own voyeuristic treatment of bodies as sites of evidence made visible through technology.

Even with this scene's disclaimer of *CSI*'s own digitalised visual style, then, the criminal's manipulation of photography, exposed by Catherine's scientifically trained eye, enacts the same kind of processing that makes the stylised look of *CSI* so visually compelling. Delhomme's crime thus raises inescapable suspicions about science's way of looking as rendered by the series's style. Once again the importation of the lab's colours to Delhomme's house in the opening of 'After the Show' is significant. For not only is the lab typically dominated by blue with greenish highlights, but the multiple layers of reflective surfaces (interior windows, glass walls, metallic surfaces, etc.) in the lab area and autopsy room settings, which help to organise the colour composition there, further create, as Lury puts it, a 'sense of both depth and transparency at a visual level', reiterating for viewers 'that the notion of "looking" itself

87

is a purposeful action' and that the lab area 'is a place of reflection as well as examination'.[53]

With looking made tantamount to knowing on CSI, it is therefore striking how 'After the Show' stylistically plays with impressions of depth and transparency, destabilising what is, for the series, the lab's visual implications of purposeful looking, of science as an act of intellectual reflection as well as empirical examination. This is why I feel that the episode exemplifies the complexity of the series's style. For what we see through the blue filter when 'After the Show' begins is Delhomme in front of a TV, reminiscent of when the CSIs stand or sit in front of a computer screen, watch the autopsy on a monitor or are visible behind the glass walls that resemble a TV screen. In our own watching him look and then turn away in profile from the screen, the act of looking – Delhomme's, the CSIs', ours as the show's viewers – is made highly problematic, since any of these perspectives confronts us with the mediation of (tele)vision by digital processing, itself an accomplishment of science.

88   CSI uses its Las Vegas setting to juxtapose the randomness of gambling with the predictability of science; but as well as being a culture of gambling, the Strip is a culture of spectacle too, as those opening shots of the Strip remind us each week, and as 'After the Show' dramatises. Yet, as the series reveals through its style, so is science, achieved through the same CGI technology of the opening shots, thereby calling into question, at least through visual analogy, the objectivity that the forensic team exemplifies in their investigation of cases. William L. Fox argues that the architecture of Las Vegas, epitomised by the casinos' use of water in their façades, their tropical motifs, their enclosed, mall-like environments, means to shut out all recognition of the city's desert origins and climate, asserting the power of the human. The sights and attractions of Las Vegas, along with its history (going back to the building of the Hoover Dam and creation of Lake Meade), testify to the imposition of human will over nature.[54] What the comparable spectacles of the Strip and Science do for CSI is to make more visible how the series's ideology of science posits the same

control and authority of culture (technology) over nature (the 'traces' of evidence that testify to the truth of a crime and never lie): the spectacle of investigation *on* the show is thus made even more riveting, in terms of the show's visual look and deployment of CGI effects to represent that technology, than the spectacle of Vegas as represented *by* the show.

6 Old and New Vegas

Whereas most crime shows on US television take place in Los Angeles or New York City, or smaller versions of the same such as San Francisco or Boston, another notable feature of *CSI* is its Las Vegas locale.

The metropolitan area of Las Vegas in Clark County boasts one of the busiest and most technically advanced forensic science labs in the USA. Even without this circumstance, a Las Vegas setting seems ready-made for a TV crime show. Las Vegas is close enough to production facilities in LA for periodic location shoots, and one city looks enough like the other in parts, so that many Southern California streets and buildings can substitute for their Vegas counterparts. Equally important to a series driven by stand-alone episodes, Las Vegas generates stories. A magnet for tourists, the setting justifies the presence of transient characters of all sorts and from all over: movie stars, sports figures, high rollers (or 'whales'), conventioneers, ordinary vacationers and couples arriving to get married.

CSI is not the first TV show to take place in Las Vegas, but the few other series set there, the older *Vega$* (1978–81) and contemporary *Las Vegas* (2003–8), limit their stories pretty much to the Strip, the locale of the famous resort complexes. Outside the city limits in an unincorporated township of Clark County named 'Paradise', the Strip began its life as the 'strip' of desert highway leading into Las Vegas from Southern California. Far-sighted entrepreneurs like Billy Wilkerson and Bugsy Siegel realised this location was the perfect spot to attract motorists before they reached the hotels and gambling halls on Fremont

Street downtown. The post-war construction of the highway's first resorts, such as the Flamingo and the Sahara, in turn led the way for the Strip's continuing development and reinvention in successive decades. In the 1950s and 60s, the ranch-style resorts along the highway had neon frontages, tropical or desert décor, and featured commercial attractions still indelibly associated with the Strip: gambling, big-name performers like Frank Sinatra and his Rat Pack pals, and lavish revues featuring topless showgirls. The present-day high-rise complexes on or just off the Strip aim to be the last word in luxury while soliciting the family trade; to supplement the gambling in their casinos and live entertainment in their theatres and nightclubs, they feature additional attractions such as spectacular themed architecture, malls with designer shops, five-star restaurants, exclusive nightclubs, and art galleries and special exhibits. The Strip is now so built up that the heavily congested automobile traffic often makes it nearly impossible to travel along what is now the southern extension of Las Vegas Boulevard.[55]

CSI by no means ignores the Strip or Clark County's economic reliance on this valuable area of real estate. Many memorable episodes begin in a location on the Strip, often the fictional Tangiers or Rampart, two casinos owned by recurring character Sam Braun. Even when crimes happen elsewhere, the glitzy, fantasy-inspired architecture of the Strip, from the Stratosphere at one end to the Luxor's pyramids at the other, seems omnipresent. The Strip is almost always a feature of the establishing shots that open each episode to announce 'Las Vegas', and then, no matter if an episode ignores the Strip completely, that distinctive skyline can usually be seen at a distance in later background shots.

If anyone epitomises Las Vegas for CSI's viewers, it is Sam Braun. He appears in just nine episodes and even then not always in a major role, but his character and the shadow it casts over the entire series bring the Strip's history to the foreground. Braun's story arc contrasts what the CSIs (and Anthony Zuiker in his DVD commentaries) refer to as 'old' Vegas circa mob control and Frank Sinatra with 'new' Vegas circa publicly traded corporations like MGM-Mirage and intricate high-tech spectacles like Cirque du Soleil.

A shot of the Strip

Due to his long involvement in the gambling industry, Braun straddles these two eras. 'He was Steve Wynn before Steve Wynn,' Grissom remarks in advance of Braun's first appearance on the series in 'Burked', which opened the second season. Catherine immediately adds, 'Oh yeah, you bet your ass. Sam came to Vegas when Vegas was dying. Built three casinos in a year. Had ties to Bugsy Siegel.'

Despite these allusions to Braun's significant role in developing new Las Vegas out of the old, 'Burked' places him in a family drama concerning the possible drug overdose of his elder son and heir. The case ultimately proves that Braun's younger son, relegated to working as a pit boss in the Tangiers and excluded from his father's will, murdered his brother when the latter reneged on a promise to split the eventual inheritance. 'I committed the cardinal sin,' Braun confesses to Catherine after the case is closed. 'I loved one son more than the other.' Braun's personal history with Catherine, whom he calls 'Mugs' and remembers as an infant, raises a suspicion, confirmed in a later episode, that he is her biological father; their blood relationship, about which she is sorely conflicted, then focuses much of the dramatic impact of his reappearances in subsequent episodes.

Catherine and Sam Braun

That focus does not mean *CSI* keeps bringing up Braun's past
as a founding father of modern Las Vegas simply to garnish the
character with a bit of local colour. Indeed, the exchange between
Grissom and Catherine in 'Burked' prepares for Braun's introduction by
establishing two central facts about him that have little to do with his
family's disintegration but have implications that the series later
expands upon: he consorted with the likes of legendary mobster Bugsy
Siegel (who opened the first upmarket resort casino, the Flamingo, in
1946) and he is the precursor of contemporary hotel magnate Steve
Wynn (who opened the Mirage, the first Vegas hotel financed through
Wall Street junk bonds, in 1989, and the Bellagio, which housed his art
collection, in 1998). As Braun's story arc develops, these two views
become more pronounced and more irreconcilable.

93

Braun's gutsy entrepreneurship in building the old-styled
Whiskey Town and Pike's Gambling Hall, then in topping them with the
swankier Tangiers and Rampart, earns respectful admiration, as
Grissom's and Catherine's comments in 'Burked' indicate. It is also the
stuff of nostalgia for the glamorous old Vegas that begat him. 'Kiss Kiss,
Bye Bye', a charming episode from season six, takes this rosy stance

toward old Vegas. Faye Dunaway guest-stars as Lois O'Neil, a retired Vegas nightclub entertainer who was herself a former Copa girl and mobster consort, is a long-time friend of Braun and has just published a tell-all autobiography promising to blow the lid off some well-kept secrets. An attempt on O'Neil's life presumably arises from what she discloses in her book, but the investigation proves she herself had arranged the hit, which the gunman bungled, in order to cover up her terminal illness; she wanted to die without tarnishing her glamorous image. Before she can be charged, O'Neil persuades her best friend – a character returning from 'Formalities' and described in that episode as 'an ex-kneebreaker' – to help her out. 'She staged her exit like a pro,' he says to Brass and Grissom afterwards, meaning she was able to leave Vegas in style.

Aside from rekindling a romance with Catherine's mother, Braun does not have much to do in this episode except to be stylish, too. He is initially a suspect in the attempt on O'Neil's life simply because one of his elegant handcrafted handkerchiefs is found on the grounds of her estate. But then the episode as a whole celebrates old Vegas for its remembered style, complete with Sinatra singing 'Almost Like Being in Love' over the teaser. And with its vivid accounts of scandalous liaisons, mobster capers and disappearances, and most of all the era's hipness and glamour, O'Neil's book stimulates Greg's romantic fascination with old Vegas; the Sinatra-like fedora he sports at this episode's end is emblematic of the lure of this mythic view of the city's past.

By this point in Braun's story arc, though, suspicions of the casino magnate's criminality are not without foundation. In counterpoint to the nostalgic tone of 'Kiss Kiss, Bye Bye', previous episodes have shown that Braun wields power in ways that recall the mob era's corruption not its style, so the hotel mogul's presence as a minor player in the O'Neil case implicitly tempers the episode's celebratory evocation of old Vegas glamour. Additionally, there are numerous references in other episodes to the Strip's mob history. Warrick, wrestling with his own gambling demons, often remembers the mobster protocols followed 'back in the day', and even Dr Robbins, all the while examining a body, sometimes mentions to his assistant or a CSI how the casino bosses used to take care of cheaters or how hit men formerly disposed of their victims. Momentarily taking on the role of Vegas historians, Warrick and Robbins reminisce about the mob's violence, lawlessness and autonomy, making the Strip of that era seem more like a throwback to Nevada's frontier days in comparison with how it operates today under the more watchful eyes of the Gaming Commission and the stock market. While there has never been any mention that Braun was actually part of the mob despite his long association with old Vegas, he acts like a mobster, or as Catherine describes it, like 'a thug in thousand dollar shoes' ('Built to Kill, Part Two').

Braun is a legend and he is ruthless. He carries into the present a gangland sense of extra-legal entitlement on his part that, it turns out, even the CSIs' science cannot touch. Two of the series's best episodes, 'Inside the Box' and 'No More Bets', build the resulting ambivalence toward his figure into their cases.

The finale of season three, 'Inside the Box' begins with an elaborately planned yet violent bank robbery whose only purpose is to retrieve a single safety-deposit box. As the investigation unfolds, evidence from this heist takes the CSIs in two directions: solving the bank robbery along with several murders that follow in its wake and reopening the cold case of a dead cocktail waitress, whose body was discovered two years earlier on the top floor of the Whiskey Town the night before its scheduled demolition. Since the murder victim in that cold case worked for Braun and the bank robbers all happen to be employees of the Rampart, Grissom and Catherine suspect that Braun somehow connects these two paths. Before the evidence officially ties the cases together, he confirms their suspicions because of the arrogance with which he avoids answering direct questions about both. When Catherine remarks that the unsolved murder at the Whiskey Town must not be good for business, Braun replies that an efficient PR department functions to bury that kind of news. 'Some things are people's business . . . some things aren't,' he states, implying that she should stay clear of his personal business – in his mind, the casinos are not only outside the city limits, but they are off limits, too.

Braun's involvement in the robbery is indirect, befitting the corporate style of running casinos: he delegates the work to someone from within the organisation hierarchy. The man who masterminds the heist and then executes his cohorts is Rob Rubio (Michael Shamus Wiles), an ex-military sharpshooter. Braun had already hired Rubio as a 'security expert' for the Rampart when some employee was suspected of skimming. Rubio's new charge is to get the safety-deposit box with no questions asked. But Braun does not stay entirely uninvolved in the heist. At around the episode's half-hour mark, he drives to a desert meeting with the surviving gunmen in order to collect the box's contents and pay them off. Metallic briefcase in hand and impeccably tailored as always, the Vegas mogul gets out of his black car and silently watches as a white car approaches. After the commercial break, Brass, Grissom and Catherine arrive at this same spot.

BRASS: Triple homicide in the desert.
GRISSOM: Old-time Vegas. We found Tommy 'the aspirin' out here. Remember him? Used to make his boss's headaches disappear.
CATHERINE: Until they made him disappear.
BRASS: I think this is the origin of the word 'termination'. There's the corporate way, and the way of the gun.

Grissom describes the triple homicide as a hit in the manner of 'old-time Vegas', and the evidence soon proves that Rubio shot the three men he arrived with before they knew what was happening and then drove away in their car. However, in confirming Braun's responsibility for the heist, that previous scene of the desert meeting encouraged the inference that his objective at this secret rendezvous was to eliminate the potential witnesses himself; in effect, Braun does just that, using Rubio to keep his own hands clean. Brass's sarcastic observation about 'termination' expands upon the 'old-time Vegas' motif, but Braun's presence at the triple slaying blurs the difference between 'the corporate

'Triple homicide in the desert'

way' and 'the way of the gun', suggesting a continuity between old and new Vegas.

The contents of the safety-deposit box (evidence incriminating Braun in the Whiskey Town murder) tell a story in the present day just as reminiscent of 'old-time Vegas'. The box belonged to the late Benny Murdock (David Selburg), whose own career followed Braun's burgeoning empire: from doorman at the Whiskey Town, to casino host at Pike's Gambling Hall, to overseeing all the gambling at the Tangiers, to acting as Braun's right-hand man on the Rampart's opening night, planned to coincide with the Whiskey Town's implosion. On that night, furious at the cocktail waitress for her infidelity with Murdock, Braun stabbed her to death with the large scissors used at the Rampart's ribbon cutting. 'Part of the old double standard,' Catherine observes, thinking no doubt both of the mob's infamous treatment of women and Braun's relation with her mother. 'No woman that you're with is ever going to be with another man.' Murdock then kept the weapon, its bloodstains storing traces of the victim and her killer, in the safety-deposit box to cover up for Braun but also presumably to hold over his head, which eventually led to their public falling out. Braun denies the charge, claiming Murdock was the guilty party and that he had learned about the scissors from Murdock just before he died. Telling Rubio 'to take care of it', Braun explains his motive for protecting Murdock's name, but what he says has even more purchase when applied to himself: 'They weren't just any pair of scissors ... they were tied to a legacy. If Benny goes down, I go down. Forty years ... building a reputation ... gone.'

At the end of 'Inside the Box', Catherine is able to make a case against Braun. However, since she compromised the blood evidence by privately using some of it for a DNA test to confirm that he is her father, in 'Assume Nothing' the court dismisses the charges. 'The guy's bullet-proof,' Warrick says with disgust when he learns what happened. Putting aside the matter of his getting away with murder, 'Inside the Box' interests me because it uses Braun's involvement in the two cases to dramatise how old and new Vegas continue to make contact. The cases contaminate 'the corporate way' of running a casino, epitomised by the sleek office where Catherine and Grissom interview Braun, with 'the way of the gun'. This theme is renewed with Braun's brief appearance in 'Assume Nothing' and again in 'Jackpot', when he sends Catherine a cheque for a quarter of a million dollars, which she cannot tear up, banking it for her daughter's future. The theme receives a more complex treatment toward the end of season four in another episode centred on Braun, 'No More Bets'.

This episode could also have been entitled 'Inside the Box'. It opens inside what used to be known as 'the box' and is now more politely referred to as 'the holding room' of a casino. A man whose face cannot be seen but whose voice identifies him to us as Sam Braun confronts a college kid suspected of cheating: 'You got any idea what we did with chumps like you back in the day?' Braun asks. When the kid defiantly says it's against the law to hold him in this room against his will, Braun adds ominously, 'There's no law in here.' With a cut to the Neon Graveyard, an empty site downtown storing the neon façades of demolished casinos, we see the kid's body tossed beneath the old Whiskey Town signage. The clues to his murder? He was killed by two shots to the back of his head but his fingers are broken, an old Vegas

99

The Neon Graveyard

method of punishing cheaters; he won over four hundred thousand dollars playing roulette at the Rampart but while no money is to be found, he still has his Rolex, so the motive cannot be robbery; and tyre-tread marks indicate that a stretch limo, of the sort Braun now travels around town in, made a three-point turn out of the area.

With its literalising allusion to 'Inside the Box', the teaser wants us to assume Braun took the kid for a ride, 'Vegas style,' as Brass comments, 'just like the old days.' But the case takes some interesting turns before reaching its conclusion. For one thing, it reveals a new high-tech way of cheating the casinos with science. The kid, Teddy Keeler (Justin Urich), had teamed up with a college buddy, Davis Mullen (Brandon Quinn), and a postgraduate engineering student, Seth Landers (Eddie Kaye Thomas), to beat the house odds with computer technology and a knowledge of physics. Put simply, Seth designed equipment that enables Davis to calibrate the forces of the spinning roulette wheel and then, through radio transmitters in their shoes, to send the calculation of where the ball will land to Teddy at the gaming table. With their huge advantage in being able to calculate the outcome moments in advance, the boys won big: first at Pike's Gambling Hall, then at the Tangiers, finally at the Rampart – all casinos owned by Braun. It therefore seems more than coincidence that Teddy was found beneath the sign of what had been Braun's first casino. When Davis's body turns up, it looks like Braun is out to retaliate against all the cheaters, but before Seth can be taken out, Brass arrests Braun for Teddy's murder.

The case reverses itself after Braun's arrest, however. First, the medical examiner determines that Davis died before Teddy. This factor challenges the timeline presumed by the CSIs, in which Braun terrorises Teddy in the box, drives him to the Neon Graveyard to kill him and catches up with Davis in the latter's apartment. Next, Warrick discovers that the targeting of Braun's casinos was purposeful and most likely personal. Earlier, Seth has explained that they chose these casinos only because they are 'old school. They're low tech. There's less interference for my gear.' Returning to the Rampart, Warrick's testing proves just the opposite, that 'the place is a mess of interference. Electronics in old casinos aren't shielded.' Finally, the CSIs learn that Seth is the son of Joe Green (Maury Chaykin), an ex-gambler with a score to settle. Years before, Braun had caught Green cheating, broken his hands as punishment and then permanently listed him in the Gaming Commission's black book, ensuring that Green could never gamble in Vegas again, not even to play the quarter slots in his neighbourhood convenience store. Using his son to set in motion a scheme to get back at Braun, Green encouraged the boys to get greedy, attracting Braun's attention. Green then saw an irresistible opportunity to frame Braun for murder when Davis phoned to tell him that Teddy had been taken to the box. As the case against Braun collapses, Green's vindictiveness is so overpowering that he leaves evidence falsely incriminating his own son for the crimes, hoping this second frame will again implicate his nemesis.

'It ceased to be about the money,' Grissom comments as the case closes and Green's guilt is determined. Since every turn of the case leads back to gambling and Sam Braun, I'm not so sure it ever ceases to be about money. Green hates Braun with so much intensity because in his mind he never cheated: 'I didn't have to cheat. I beat the casinos. I beat 'em, and they ganged up on me . . .' 'No,' Brass corrects him, 'you beat Sam Braun's casino and he ended your gambling career. . . . That sounds like motive to me.' Furthermore, 'No More Bets' closes with Seth Landers accepting Braun's patronage. 'Right,' Catherine observes when she sees Seth riding with Sam in the luxurious stretch limo, 'he gets to work off his debt.' 'You want to catch a cheat, hire one,' Braun explains, adding, with as much reference to Catherine (and the cheque she cashed) as to Seth, 'One way or another, I always get my money's worth.'

Clearly, the episode proves the axiom that money is power in Vegas. The gambling industry not only drives the economy but it inspires the greed feeding this economy, which is why the science used in the cheating scheme can be so easily co-opted – by the college boys to begin with, then by Green, then by Braun. And as much as it has to do with his wise-guy tactics, Braun's longevity in Vegas results from his ability as a casino operator to keep up with the changing times and

101

continue to profit from the gambling industry. Hence, in the coda, he hires Seth to get his 'money's worth' from the latter's knowledge of the new technology.

'The way of the gun' finally catches up with Braun at the start of season seven, and it does so because of his 'corporate way' of modernising his casino holdings. In the two-part 'Built to Kill', an investor in the Eclipse, a brand-new Braun hotel and casino to be built on the site of the imploded Rampart, kills himself when the project's financing falls through and he loses twenty million dollars. Always knowing how to get his 'money's worth', Braun regroups with a new stock issue and comes out ahead. In retaliation, the unlucky investor's male partner/lover and brother team up to avenge the suicide with a somewhat far-fetched scheme (the two men make Catherine think she was drugged and raped, and then kidnap her daughter) to torment Braun while extorting the lost twenty million from him. When the scheme fails, the dead man's lover kills Braun in front of his casino, proving that the Vegas tycoon is not bullet-proof after all.

Sam Braun's story arc contributes to the series's mythification of 'old Vegas' but, as his first and final appearances indicate, his impact

Sam Braun is shot and dies in his daughter's arms

also tends to be personalised, turned into domestic drama and folded into Catherine's backstory. Nonetheless, that should not distract from how his figure amplifies for *CSI* the popular mystique of Las Vegas as 'Sin City' through its mob history. For condensed into Braun's biography is a larger picture of the Strip's emergence from mob-controlled casinos into sprawling theme-park hotels owned by a handful of large corporations and financed by Wall Street.

To be sure, Braun's story arc simplifies the stages through which 'old' Vegas was transformed into the 'new'. For instance, *CSI*'s repeated citations of this old/new binary eliminates reference both to Howard Hughes, who commandeered the Desert Inn in the mid-1960s and then began purchasing as many other properties as he could, and to Hughes's Summa Corporation's development (through various land transfers) after his death of master-planned communities in Summerlin (named after Hughes's grandmother).[56] Hughes's impact on the Strip was transformational. His company took control of casinos from mob-related interests on one hand and fought the Justice Department's intervention in his growing portfolio on the other, so his personal and corporate presence on the Strip marks a stage in its history that comes between what *CSI* considers 'old' and 'new' Vegas. In fact, given Braun's approximate age, that time in the past 'when Vegas was dying', as Catherine recalls, is probably when he began his career with the Whiskey Town, making him a contemporary of Hughes as well as a cohort of Bugsy Siegel and a rival of Steve Wynn.[57]

Braun's Rampart Hotel and Casino marks another sort of referential instability in his story arc. I always have the impression from how it is handled in the series that the fictional Rampart is, like the fictional Tangiers, located on the Strip. Yet on more than one occasion its address is given as the Resorts of Summerlin, where an actual Rampart casino exists. Could this be the introduction of an element of 'realism' on the writers' part, much like local TV journalist Paula Francis's appearances whenever *CSI* shows a news programme, as in 'After the Show'? Possibly. But when Braun's Rampart is imploded to make way for the new Eclipse in 'Built to Kill, Part One', the imagery does place the demolished complex on the Strip, at least according to the surrounding buildings. Like the bigger ellipses mentioned above, this ambiguity is symptomatic of the tricky and selective way *CSI* negotiates Las Vegas history through Sam Braun's figure. His story arc invests the past with its mythic aura, and in this way romanticises it as a history detached from the modern-day era of the Strip's corporate ownership, but the arc also registers the continuing impact of gambling on Clark County's economic development.

7 What Happens in Vegas

For all its contemporary redevelopment, the Strip still capitalises on the mystique of Las Vegas as 'Sin City'. The clichéd advertising slogan 'What happens in Vegas . . . stays in Vegas', which *CSI* and the network's promotion sometimes reference, creates an impression that the city is perpetual Mardi Gras. Lured there by the combined promises of instant wealth in the casinos and legitimate or less reputable opportunities for sexual gratification in the many large and small clubs, visitors to 'Sin City' have implicit permission to retreat from or even break the rules of daily life, indulge in conventional or unorthodox pleasures, and not give a thought to the consequences.

 CSI spins the 'Sin City' cliché, taking it literally and with some irony. As the other side of the presumption that Las Vegas relaxes the various constraints defining everyday life, what happens in the city does indeed stay there when it results in a crime that the CSIs investigate. After all, can anything be more permanent and consequential than ending up in Doc Robbins's morgue? But the more interesting way in which *CSI* spins the cliché's truthfulness results from all the attention given to the area's residents. Whether making the point explicitly or not, most *CSI* cases end up reflecting upon how Las Vegas is a 21st-century metropolis with a cultural ethos all its own that leaves a distinctive imprint upon the lives of those who live and work there.

With the Strip so entrenched as the symbol of Las Vegas, the city seems inseparable from tourism, so *CSI*'s relative disinterest in this side of Vegas stands out immediately. Whenever a case involves tourists, it is usually because they naively take to heart the cliché about Vegas and find themselves in serious trouble. These situations, moreover, typically form the basis of an episode's secondary plot. Recall from the first season the middle-aged man in 'Pilot' who gets drugged and robbed by a hooker. 'I . . . I love my wife,' he explains to Nick. 'We've been married thirty-one years now. I've never cheated on her before. I come into town for this convention and I'm sitting in the lounge minding my own business, when this sweet-smelling brunette came up to me and next thing I know, she's nibbling on my earlobe.' After a brief flashback interrupts his account, he adds with a nod to Nick, 'and for a second there, I thought I was your age again'.

Or remember from that same season the drunken bride-to-be in 'To Halve and to Hold'. Thinking 'I'm in Vegas, it doesn't really count', she has sex with the male stripper hired for her bachelorette party only to see her fiancé bludgeon the man to death in a jealous rage when he breaks in on them. 'We just . . . we just were hoping we could get married. Put it all behind us,' the prospective groom bemoans when confronted with the evidence of his crime. 'Laws don't end when you come to Vegas,' Warrick sternly reminds him.

Then there is the gambler in 'Cool Change', also from season one, who reluctantly plays a slot machine because his girlfriend has a 'premonition'. Unexpectedly winning the forty million dollar jackpot, he callously dumps her, so she just as coolly slams a heavy candlestick into his head and throws his body off the balcony of the Presidential Suite in an attempt to make his death look like a suicide. 'How are you so cool?' Nick asks the woman after Grissom presents the evidence against her. 'You took someone's life. Don't you care?' 'No,' she replies.

Sometimes the presence of tourists turns out to be incidental to the crime, whether because they happen upon the scene accidentally, make a lucky escape or are innocent victims. 'Viva Las Vegas', the season five opener, seeks to re-establish the narrative presence of the series's setting according to the DVD commentary, and to do so it intentionally recalls situations and dialogue from 'Pilot'. One such instance is the case involving a golf ball salesman. He awakens in his Palermo Hotel room next to a dead stripper, both their bodies covered in blood. Suspicion immediately falls on the tourist and then on the stripper's boyfriend, who knew that she turned tricks after hours; yet the evidence collected by Catherine discloses that this death was not foul play but instead resulted from an accidental fall in the bathroom. Having previously drugged her hapless trick, the stripper failed to rouse him when, bleeding profusely and seeking assistance, she crawled back to the bed but then collapsed on top of him and died.

'Viva Las Vegas' is one of those occasional *CSI* episodes to feature four cases, the rest of which depict the city on a larger canvas: a killing in a dance club north of downtown, which leads to another body in a well-appointed private residence; a bathtub electrocution in a cheap downtown residential motel; and the unearthing of what looks like the corpse of an alien in the outlying desert not far from the notorious Area 51. As in the case of the stripper's death, the evidence solves these cases with the expected *CSI* twist. The club shooting raises the question of how anyone could smuggle a gun past the metal detector at the entrance. The murder, Grissom and Greg's investigation reveals, was committed by an employee: she stole the revolver from the desk of the club's co-owner and concealed it inside a toilet, so that it never had to pass through the security check after all. It seems the woman was desperate to extricate herself from the club's other owner, who had used her to smuggle drugs and was now threatening her life if she talked in order to avoid a jail term. Convinced that it was imprisonment or death, she hired a hit man to eliminate her problem; but upon the job's completion, he doubled his price. Unable to find the money to pay him off, she decided that her only way out was to kill him, knowing the club's noise would muffle the gunfire.

In the meantime, Warrick learns that the electrocuted man was a down-and-out compulsive gambler, formerly of Phoenix, who finally hit a big jackpot at the Golden Nugget. On his way back to his room, he bragged about turning his life around to a kid selling hot dogs on the street. The young vendor, equally addicted to gambling everyday but with nothing to show for it, followed the winner to the motel and broke into his room. Surprised in the bathtub, the winner refused to disclose his money's whereabouts, so the hot-dog guy tossed a live radio into the water, found the stash hidden in a Bible and spent much of it on high-end electronic equipment.

And as for that alien? This case leads Nick and Sara to Vegas's themed wedding chapels. Some time back, one chapel owner, an Elvis Presley impersonator, found the body of his competitor, who performed weddings in the guise of an extraterrestial, and took the still-costumed corpse for a proper burial as close as possible to Area 51. Then the only reasonable course of action, the man explains, was to take over the dead rival's business, alternating between marrying couples in one chapel dressed as Elvis and in the other as ET. According to the evidence, however, that dead man was not dead after all but subject to a rare medical condition that gave his body the appearance of a corpse; he was actually buried alive.

Although these four cases differ in tone, producer Carol Mendelsohn states on the DVD that 'Viva Las Vegas' includes 'stories that could only be told in Vegas'. In one way or another, the cases dramatise hopeful schemes suddenly turning into desperate acts. Taken together, the stories represent Las Vegas as a culture harbouring misfits, characters who gravitated to the city and got stuck there because they don't belong or can't survive anywhere else. The characters in each story are mostly minor players in the city's tourist economy; they hardly benefit from its prosperity and growth, and, having missed the gravy train, inhabit a shady grey area when it comes to respectability and the law. The four stories, in other words, could 'only be told in Vegas' because they refract the city through the tourist industry's impact on characters who in differing ways reside at its margins and get stuck there: working in a service capacity for this industry, exploiting it, victimised by it.

CSI may not overly dwell on the tourist's Las Vegas but this does not mean it views the city and its culture as entirely separable from that lucrative industry, even though the connection, as I've begun to suggest, is often made indirectly the further one travels from the Strip. Cases often show that residents get involved in crimes, innocently or not, because, like the tourists gravitating to 'Sin City', they think of Vegas as a utopian idea, an oasis in the desert (in Spanish, 'Las Vegas' means 'the meadows') where they can strike it rich or reinvent themselves. William L. Fox explains the phenomenon of Vegas's appeal to the imagination in this way:

> As a species we're not well equipped to function in the desert. We lose our sense of physical scale and perspective in such landscapes, which opens a gap between what we think we are seeing and the reality. And the Strip exploits that gap as far as our imaginations will allow.
>
> The greater the dissonance between perception and reality, the more extreme our cultural responses become in order to compensate. The Mojave Desert is one of the most arid places on the planet, and Las Vegas therefore a correspondingly strong presence in it.[58]

As manifestations of that 'strong presence', Fox has in mind the audacious spectacles orchestrated by the casino-hotels in their architecture and décor, particularly in the ways they include water, and in their high-tech shows, museums and galleries, and exotic animal exhibits. Furthermore, he maintains that the imposition of 'culture' over 'nature' in response to the desert's disorienting effect on perception is not limited to the Strip, since the same logic of spectacle, of 'the complicated overlaying of materials and images until they overwhelm the senses', can be found throughout the city, even in non-commercial venues.[59] *CSI* views the 'strong presence' of Las Vegas in somewhat the same terms. The series focuses in particular on the 'dissonance between perception and reality' that the Strip's commodification of fantasy epitomises but that also characterises Las Vegas culture as a whole, at least as *CSI* depicts it. To illustrate, I want to look at 'Time of Your Death', one of the few episodes devoted entirely to a case involving a tourist.

In 'Time of Your Death', as a reward for noticing and correcting an unfavourable clause that saves him millions of dollars in his divorce settlement, movie producer Mick Sheridan (Judd Nelson) gives his assistant Jeff Powell (Kyle Howard) the corporate Visa card and sends him to Las Vegas 'to have some fun'. Upon his arrival at the Palermo Hotel and Casino, Powell meets a sexy but unhappy blonde (Julie Benz). They strike up a conversation at the bar, during which she accidentally spills her drink all over him, begins to cry and points to her abusive millionaire lover playing baccarat in the distance.

Powell comforts her and she responds with equal warmth. To make up for spoiling his clothes, the blonde buys him an expensive leather suit in one of the hotel's designer shops. Then the couple takes her red Ferrari to the Cue-T, an off-Strip pool hall, where, before a cheering crowd, Powell wins ten thousand dollars. Driving her Ferrari, Powell takes the blonde back to the Palermo. The man who lost all that money to Powell in the pool game angrily follows the couple in his Corvette. The Ferrari and the Corvette engage in a high-speed race, and Powell wins this competition, too.

After Powell and the blonde return to his room, the two celebrate and have sex. As she drifts off to sleep, he slips out of the room. Head over heels in love, Powell intends to use his winnings to surprise the blonde with an expensive bracelet from the Palermo jewellery store next to the casino. But first, exhilarated by his unbelievable luck all evening and consequently emboldened by a feeling of invincibility, he stops at the baccarat tables. Powell confronts the blonde's former paramour, telling him, 'she doesn't need you or your money any more, man. That's right. Because she has everything she needs now – love and respect. So you go ahead and play your little card game. All right? 'Cause you the playa. But I'm the man. The man.' Shortly afterwards, 'the man' is found dead on the Palermo's loading dock, and the case begins for the CSIs.

From this reconstructed timeline of what happens prior to the body's discovery, it seems as if Vegas's culture of chance – in the triple sense of 'luck', 'opportunity' and 'risk' – makes it possible for an

Jeff Powell has the time of his life

ordinary guy like Jeff Powell to experience what he cannot achieve in his normal life: attract a sexy blonde, win a great deal of money in a pool game, race in a red Ferrari. Powell's exciting night on the town, however, does not just happen by chance. It turns out that his employer arranged for Caprice Unlimited – a local company whose motto is 'anything is possible' – to stage a fantasy scenario as part of this

The script

all-expenses-paid vacation in Las Vegas. The script, 'meticulously planned in advance' and written out in detail for all participants but Powell, draws on his long-time hobby of pool-playing, his interest in NASCAR racing, his shyness around beautiful women and his inclination to be a knight in shining armour. The blonde herself is a professional gambler and the other pool player is a former stunt-car driver, both hired by Caprice for this scenario; the expensive sports cars they drive were leased for the evening, too. According to Caprice's script, the staged fantasy is supposed to end outside Powell's hotel room. The blonde has the option of going inside at this point, but her instructions state she must assume full responsibility for her decision if that happens.

The blonde's willingness to go 'off script' with Powell does not cause his death, as one might surmise. Rather, earlier in the evening a chance event not anticipated by Caprice's script intrudes upon the scenario's careful isolation of reality from its illusionism. Powell mistakes a real person for the blonde's fictional lover. Although the script tells her to gesture toward no one in particular as she complains about her rich but abusive lover, Powell wrongly thinks she points to Dennis Kim (Will Yun Lee), an arrogant Korean millionaire and one of the Palermo's regular 'whales'. When Powell confronts him hours later, Kim has absolutely no idea what the man is going on about and assumes he is drunk or crazy. Kim's two bodyguards follow Powell and, intending only to beat the man up when he returns from the jewellery store, they accidentally kill him. The bodyguards probably thought they were just teaching Powell a lesson, Catherine surmises, and Grissom agrees: 'They did: don't confuse fantasy with reality.'

In its meticulous planning of this anonymous 'gift', Caprice Unlimited organises the scenario as if it were an elaborate and invisible amusement-park ride; the evening's simulated experience will be thrilling for Powell but the scenario, its staged fantasy based on his personality profile yet the handiwork of someone else, is designed to be over as soon as it reaches its scripted ending. For Powell, however, the scenario is so intoxicating that he gets high on it, overestimating his sense of personal and physical empowerment, and this illusion of autonomy is ultimately the fantasy that victimises him the most. The blonde is a reputable gambler and not a prostitute, yet Powell is her 'trick' in the sense that he is fooled by the oldest trick in the book as far as Vegas goes. 'You know, the biggest fantasy in Vegas', Nick states in the conclusion, 'is that everything here happens by chance. Nothing here happens by chance. The odds are set before you get off the plane.'

Nick obviously has in mind the betting odds in a casino, which are always in the house's favour, although his observation applies equally well to the controls set on fantasy by the sex industry. Furthermore, in speaking as both a resident and a CSI, Nick's statement carries the added weight of his being an observer of Vegas. Just as the logic of science trumps the apparent randomness of chance, enabling the criminologist to discern how a single unexpected event insinuated itself into the scenario's meticulous planning, so too this inhabitant of Las Vegas sees the city's logic differently from the tourists. He does not confuse the fantasy of 'Sin City' with the reality of Las Vegas, yet well understands the ease with which the two can become conflated for the naive visitor like Jeff Powell. Caprice Unlimited's business may only be affordable to an elite clientele but it typifies how the city's commerce traffics in fantasy, from Anthony Caprice himself to the locals, such as the blonde and the pool player, whom Caprice hires, and why consumers buy it. The fantasy on sale is the utopian yet illusory vision of Las Vegas as an oasis of freedom and fulfilment in the desert.

Thematically, 'Time of Your Death' recalls a very popular episode from season two, 'Slaves of Las Vegas', which also deals with Vegas's commodification of fantasy yet has little to do with tourism. This episode opens with a young couple making out in the sandpit of a neighbourhood park; they discover buried there the body of Mona Taylor (Nicola Hindshaw), which leads the CSIs first to a plastic surgeon specialising in breast implants and then to a large restored and isolated Victorian house: Lady Heather's Dominion. Lady Heather (Melinda Clarke) runs an S/M fetish club aimed at a clientele that includes city officials and wealthy residents. For a sizeable fee, these men enact their fantasies of dominating or submitting to women.

Lady Heather's Dominion is one of those highly successful (she clears twenty grand a week) Las Vegas enterprises that, taking full advantage of the city's capacity to exploit sexual fantasy, finds a

The CSIs arrive outside Lady Heather's Dominion

ready-made customer base of locals and so does not cater to tourists. Visually resembling an old-time brothel, the house is a special retreat where, indulging their fantasies, her clients can bring them 'to life' yet return home afterwards with the liquid latex washed off and the whips put away. Managed by Lady Heather with skill, finesse and an expert ability to read her clients' desires, this unorthodox establishment sells an interactive form of sexual theatre not too different from the erotic spectacle on view and for sale in the Strip's nightclubs and floorshows or the less respectable versions available in the strip joints and lap-dancing clubs located off the Strip and nearer to downtown. As Lady Heather explains to Grissom, 'some men go to the theatre, some men are the theatre. Either way, what I offer is a chance for submission or control, whichever's required.' Moreover, she insists that the service she provides has an underlying social and psychological basis in 'reality'.

'What happens here isn't about violence,' she further comments to Grissom. 'It's about challenging preconceived notions of Victorian normalcy. Bringing people's fantasies to life. Making them real and acceptable.' Her establishment makes fantasies 'real' in so far as it provides a space where they can be actualised as living theatre, and the activity being staged expresses desires that, due to social regulation, are considered inexpressible.

     Although Lady Heather describes her establishment as a form of theatre, her dominion is not entirely a setting for 'play'. In acting out those challenges to 'normalcy', this living theatre leaves real scars on real bodies, as Mona Taylor's corpse displays. Likewise, the old Victorian house may be spatially as well as architecturally removed from the otherwise ordinary lives of those patronising the fetish club, but Mona's death exposes how the patrons' normalcy cannot be insulated from what Lady Heather's theatre achieves in 'bringing people's fantasies to life'. For while the crime itself took place in one of her subterranean chambers, the motive for it leads the CSIs to a highly troubled marriage in a wealthy residential community, significantly filmed in bright daylight in contrast with the first night-time views of Lady Heather's Dominion. In their comfortable suburban home, Eileen

Lady Heather

and Cameron Nelson (Kelly Rowan and Mitchell Whitfield) seem like your average, post-feminist, upper-middle-class couple. She works as a high-powered attorney, while he serves as their child's primary caretaker. But Eileen is cold, dominating and castrating; submissive in the marital relationship, Cameron hires Mona, who is working off the books at Lady Heather's, as a surrogate for his wife. Inverting the sadomasochist roles structuring his marriage, he forces Mona even to beg for oxygen (which is how she dies).

This case's resolution in suburbia is very typical of *CSI*. Regular viewers may realise, and unlike the franchise's two spin-offs, that *CSI* pays a great deal of attention to domestic crime in Las Vegas. In the first three seasons alone, 'Blood Drops', 'Sex, Lies and Larvae', 'Fahrenheit 932', 'To Halve and to Hold', 'Gentle, Gentle', 'Justice Is Served', 'Burked', 'Overload', 'Organ Grinder', 'The Finger', 'Abra-Cadaver', 'Recipe for Murder', 'Got Murder?', 'One Hit Wonder', 'Lucky Strike', 'Crash and Burn', 'Last Laugh' and 'Forever' all feature A or B plots in which one family member (a spouse, a child, a sibling, a lover)

Grissom and Catherine interrogate the Camerons

causes the death of another, whether intentionally or not. This impromptu list does not include cases connecting to domestic life more indirectly, such as those involving high-schoolers, neighbours, home invasion and business associates who take their quarrels out of the office.

117

The concentration on domestic crimes helps *CSI* to sketch the economic transformation of Las Vegas from a small gambling town into the sprawling metropolis of Clark County. As well as being 'an intense locus of financial activity in the middle of one of the world's most severe deserts', Metropolitan Las Vegas is a landscape of planned communities imposed upon that arid and inhospitable terrain.[60] The Las Vegas of *CSI* likewise extends past the Strip and the downtown core to encompass self-contained housing developments such as Summerlin, located northwest of the Strip and miles away from the urban centre; independent cities that have become bedroom suburbs such as Henderson and Boulder City (originally built by the US government to serve the Hoover Dam); and recreational areas such as Lake Meade, the artificial lake resulting from the construction of the Hoover Dam in the 1930s, Red Rock Canyon and of course the Mojave Desert – these are all settings of various *CSI* cases.

A view of Vegas as mass housing development

Furthermore, along with its diverse geography, metropolitan Las Vegas has a heterogeneous population whose growth has far outpaced the urban infrastructure. As already noted, most cases on *CSI* involve these locals, and the crimes occur far away from the hotel-casinos on the Strip: in private estates, gated communities, upscale apartment complexes and condominiums, rundown motels or trailer parks; in 24-hour supermarkets, mom and pop groceries, elite restaurants, coffee shops or dance clubs; in places of worship, high schools or the university campus; in silver mines, construction sites and businesses having nothing to do with tourism or gambling. For the area's residents, the Strip is not a tourist attraction but their local leisure destination, the place to go out to dinner, to see a movie or show, to shop, to socialise at a bar or club, and to try their luck at the slot machines or gaming tables. As a matter of course on *CSI*, we often see locals, including members of the CSI team, patronising the shops and restaurants on the Strip, gambling there, or even picking up sex partners, but they are not on holiday – rather, the Strip is just one part of their everyday life as inhabitants of this urban environment.

Likewise, the Strip thrives on multitudes of tourists but its businesses rely on a very large workforce – showgirls on stage, valets in the car parks, cleaners toiling behind the scene in the hotels – who reside in Las Vegas and make up its working class, the large labour force needed to keep the numerous hotels, motels, restaurants, clubs and casinos running. Vegas, in fact, has been called 'the last Detroit' according to Hal Rothman, because it is 'the most unionized city in the United States'.[61] While many workers make a good living because of their union, the comfortable upper-middle-class suburban life far from the Strip in the many walled-in, generically planned gated communities exists in stark contrast with the much less prosperous Hispanic, African-American and, to a lesser extent, Asian populations increasingly dispossessed and unempowered by Las Vegas's economic expansion.

CSI does not minimise this side of Vegas, whether to highlight the racial tensions that exist between the police and residents, as in 'A Bullet Runs through It, Parts One and Two', or to explore inside an ethnic community, as in the narcocorrido music subculture of 'Snakes'. More commonly, though, *CSI* maps the diverse cultural geography of Las Vegas in the less obvious manner of 'Slaves of Las Vegas'. Its secondary plot concerns an armed robbery of a Hispanic neighbourhood cheque-cashing store owned by Carla Delgado (Tracy Vilar) and her brother, who was shot by one of the gunmen. When Sara tries to calm the victim down by saying she knows Carla is upset, the latter replies, showing how she is the cultural opposite of the cool, legalistic Eileen Cameron: 'Upset? Upset is for white people, lady. I'm pissed off.' This crime turns domestic, too. Carla's husband, Hector (Amaury Nolasco), was one of the thieves, and the brother-in-law whom he shot was, in turn, skimming the store's cash. When both crimes are disclosed, Carla wants Sara to haul the men's asses off to jail where she hopes they will have to stay for a long time. This economically and ethnically distinctive locale, in sum, indicates a different instance of

Warrick and Sara investigate the robbery in the Delgados's store

'what happens in Vegas', which counterpoints the primary plot's movement from Lady Heather's Dominion to the Nelsons's suburban household.

In displaying this social stratification, *CSI* repeatedly emphasises the singularity of Las Vegas as a culture of difference on all fronts. Sara asks a potential witness to the Delgado robbery if he has seen anything unusual, and the man replies matter-of-factly, 'in Las Vegas, unusual is what happens when you leave the house'. With the Strip as its nucleus and inspiration, Las Vegas is an unusual setting indeed, because, in provoking visitors and residents to break the rules of everyday life, it inspires unorthodox behaviour in all sorts of ways – nothing can be more out of the ordinary than Lady Heather's Dominion. But as 'Slaves of Las Vegas' also illustrates, *CSI* simultaneously views Las Vegas as an ordinary setting, because, apart from the wealth and fantasy that the Strip displays, crime, as it refracts the city and its environs, turns out to be rather banal in its motivation. Whether taking the form of rage (the Mona Taylor death) or greed (the Delgado store robbery), the frequent turns to domestic crime on *CSI* reveal that, no matter how perverse its execution or bizarre its discovery, and in contrast with a tendency on the Miami and New York spin-offs to go way over the top when inventing cases related to their settings, crime on *CSI* remains human in its size and scale, and the same is true of the series's Las Vegas.

CSI's attention to domestic crimes can be considered generic of television in so far as it gives expression to cultural anxieties about the status and safety of the middle-class family while giving the crimes an appearance of universality. But when contextualised in the series's setting, the idea of domestic criminality also functions in a more specific and concrete relation to Vegas's fantasy reputation as 'Sin City'. Often beginning on a bizarre note, the crimes on *CSI* implicitly measure the locals of Clark County, many of whom are striving to achieve an upper-middle-class suburban lifestyle despite the aura of the Strip, against the tourists and gamblers, purposefully gravitating there, eager to escape a middle-class life back home, willing to risk its comforts and stability, by immersing themselves in the pleasures offered up by the Strip. As 'Slaves of Las Vegas' exemplifies, the domestic crimes register Las Vegas's impact on middle-class 'normalcy'. These cases dramatise the connection between what otherwise appears to be the insulated fantasy world of 'Sin City', where 'anything is possible' and people can have the time of their life (or death), and the equally insulated 'real' world of everyday domestic life in Las Vegas, where perverse desires, ordinarily regulated by social and moral convention, break free and make their impact felt with disturbing violence.

121

8 Who Are You?

CSI's view of crime and its motivations is well summarised by a remark Grissom makes at one point in 'A Little Murder', an episode from season three that takes place at the annual convention of the International Organisation of Little People (IOLP). As Dr Robbins shows him signs of painful bone-lengthening surgery performed on a dwarf's body many years before, Grissom sadly observes, 'what people will endure to be normal'. His statement could supply an appropriate epitaph for almost any episode of *CSI*. Case after case reveals that people will go to extreme lengths to be considered normal; they commit terrible acts in their efforts to hide their secrets or they find themselves in desperate straits once the restrictions of being normal push them beyond their threshold of endurance.

To be sure, many episodes make this revelation indirectly. In some chilling episodes, such as 'What's Eating Gilbert Grissom?' and 'After the Show', *CSI* asks us to witness along with the investigating team the monstrousness of serial killers and rapists, and to pass judgment on their heinous acts. From this perspective, *CSI* shares a thematic concern with *Law and Order: Special Victims Unit* (1999–), another series that pushes the envelope when it comes to representing perverse and horrific acts. On *SVU*, the legal and juridical institutions, portrayed as sincerely trying to serve and protect sexual victims, obey the statutes and so define the standards that differentiate normality from abnormality. *CSI*, on the other hand, more often than not makes a point of showing that 'normal' is a fragile category. The Blue Paint Killer remains at large when 'The Execution of Catherine Willows' closes because, as Grissom mutters over a shot of an anonymous crowd, the killer can hide in plain sight: 'he must've looked like he belonged . . . like the insects, he blended in'. And when Kevin Greer is finally apprehended in 'What's Eating Gilbert Grissom?', he asks Grissom and Brass if they wished he looked scarier. The killer's average appearance, which had enabled him to blend in with the crowd, belies his monstrous acts. One can say much the same about benign first impressions of the average middle-class family, only seemingly endangered by some outside force as it turns out, in 'Blood Drops', 'Gentle, Gentle', 'Feeling the Heat' and 'Harvest'. In 'Identity Crisis', Judge Douglas Mason, aka serial killer Paul Millander, even invites Grissom to his house for a family supper with his wife and son!

More than science, then, a continuing interrogation of normalcy turns the ethical compass of *CSI*. It determines the character of the crimes, while affecting the characterisation of the CSI team, Grissom in particular, which accounts for the series's abiding interest in unconventional behaviour, desires, bodies and social networks. Indeed, if the Vegas setting were to add nothing else to the series, it would still encourage an elastic understanding of normalcy, plainly evident in those 'stories that can only be told in Vegas'.

123

Recall, for instance, the plushies and furries convention in 'Fur and Loathing'. This gathering at the King's River Hotel establishes a safe space for 'a whole tribe of people who prefer to interact as furry animals rather than human beings', as Grissom describes the 'fascinating' congregation. Not bothered by outside regulation or interference, the persons attending PAF CON inhabit alternative identities symbolised by their costumes (raccoon, lamb, kitten, wolf, etc.). Their organisation as a social unit, moreover, forms the basis of a 'tribe' according to Grissom, a community with its own sexual protocols such as 'skritching' and 'yiffing' in a 'furpile'. The tribal affiliation legitimates what, to the normal world, seems odd, quirky, humorous or bizarre behaviour. 'This is weirding me out,' Catherine says when she and Grissom first arrive at the convention, so he explains to her, 'It's not that weird. It's instinctual.' To illustrate, he

Catherine and Grissom at PAF CON

compares the 'furry' attire first with the bearskins worn by native American tribes, then with Jungian archetypes.

124   While Grissom's fascination determines the non-judgmental stance that this episode takes toward the plushies and furries phenomenon, the other members of his team remain 'weirded out' by it. Greg, for instance, who's ordinarily knowledgeable of and interested in all things subcultural, like the sexual uses of latex in 'Slaves of Las Vegas', refers to the deceased as a 'manimal' and a 'schmohawk'. 'I don't get this whole thing,' Warrick also says of the furry lifestyle. 'It's Vegas,' Catherine replies, adding somewhat too glibly: 'People come here to be animals.' The CSIs' hostility to the furries lets the team act as a surrogate for an audience who may respond similarly to this strange subculture, but that dismissive attitude also prevents the team from solving the case sooner than they do.

That is because normalcy itself can be described as the culprit in this episode. First, and related to what I discussed in the previous chapter, all the 'furries' interviewed in this case appear to be locals, not conventioneers. Second, and more to my point now, the 'crime', if one can call it that, begins when the man who thinks of himself as 'Rocky

Racoon' (Evan Arnold) has a fight with his lover, 'Linda Lamb' (Traci L. Crouch). Assuming he has fallen off the wagon when in fact he has been drugged by a rival for her affections, she kicks 'Rocky Racoon' out of the car. He feels sick, so he kneels down on the side of the road, vomits and is shot, mistaken for a coyote by the rancher who lives atop the hillside. 'Linda Lamb', meanwhile, has a change of heart and drives back to fetch her stranded boyfriend. She swerves to avoid hitting him as he crawls, fatally wounded, into the middle of the road, and she slams into an oncoming truck. 'We took one look at those furry suits and thought foul play,' Catherine concludes at the end of this episode, 'but this was really a domestic dispute gone mad.'

Grissom, needless to say, serves as the ethical as well as intellectual leader of the CSIs because he most vocally recognises that 'normal' and 'natural' are not interchangeable terms and that, as a consequence, the social body and the physical body are often in conflict. 'Hey, if the world doesn't adapt itself to you, you have to adapt yourself to it, right?' he says to Melanie Grace (Meredith Eaton) when, interviewing her at the little people's convention, he admires her reaching tool in 'A Little Murder'. Playing the slot machines right after finding a friend's corpse may seem cold-hearted, so Melanie explains: 'This is the convention. Everything happens at warp speed. . . . You know, fifty-one weeks in your hometown with nothing but average-sized people. I have to fit a lifetime into this week. We all do. Business connections, gambling, romance.' The week in Las Vegas temporarily relieves Melanie of the burden of conformity; in the past, her hometown life had led her to internalise the negation of her own difference from everyone else. 'My first IOLP convention,' she continues, warming up to Grissom because of his sincere interest, 'I walk in, see two hundred dwarves staring back at me and what goes through my head? "There's no way I look like these people." I ran.' 'But you went back,' Grissom notes. 'Eventually,' she continues. 'I guess I realised it's nice to see eye-to-eye with someone.'

When Grissom responds only with 'mmm', Melanie observes, 'I get the impression that's a little tough for you.' In elaboration, she

125

Melanie Grace

quotes Carson McCullers: 'The freaks have looked at her in a secret way and tried to connect their eyes with hers as though to say, we know who you are. We are you.' Grissom smiles, because Melanie is right. 'I think we look for the differences in each other to prove that we're not alone,' he comments.

As dramatised by 'Fur and Loathing' and 'A Little Murder', normalcy on *CSI* turns out to be a social fiction and crime marks that fiction's breaking point. Explaining to Grissom that her small size is the result of a random gene, Melanie confesses, 'Sometimes I've even seen terror in average-size people's eyes. I remind them that their little carbon copies might not be such a copy after all.' Her statement neatly condenses the crime in this episode, too: a dwarf with an average-sized daughter kills her fiancé, who is also a dwarf, to stop them from marrying and having children; ironically, the daughter is already pregnant. 'You know what's really sad?' Grissom states as the murderer is taken away. 'This wasn't just a murder. It was a hate crime.'

Grissom's fascination with difference, a reflection of his own sense of being 'freakish', as Melanie senses, supplies the continuity for cases involving physical deviations from normalcy (in addition to 'Little

Murder', for instance, 'Sounds of Silence' concerns the deaf community, 'Caged' pivots around an autistic witness, the victim in 'The Hunger Artist' suffers from anorexia and bulimia, and her sister from schizophrenic paranoia, the victim and his sister in 'Werewolves' have hypertrichosis or 'human werewolf syndrome', etc.) and those introducing the CSIs to alternative lifestyles or unorthodox subcultures (along with the plushies and furries in 'Fur and Loathing', there are the S/M fetish club in 'Slaves of Las Vegas' and its sequel, 'Lady Heather's Box', the goth vampires in 'Suckers', the fetish biter in 'Bite Me', the diaper fetishist in 'King Baby', the Buddhist monks in 'Felonious Monk', the Sherlock Holmes club in 'Who Shot Sherlock?', the male corset wearer in 'Way to Go', etc.). 'Ch-Ch-Changes', the series's milestone 100th episode, well represents this continuing theme.

Wendy Garner (Sarah Buxton), the murdered male-to-female transsexual showgirl in 'Ch-Ch-Changes', desperately wants to keep her fiancé from learning about her preoperative life as a biological male; she goes so far as to plant indications of menstrual blood in her bathroom in order to appear physically normal to him. Wendy's psychologist, Dr Mona Lavelle (Lindsay Crouse), is sincere in her desire to help transsexuals whose requests for surgery are rejected by the medical establishment. These good intentions aside, because of her insufficient expertise and inadequate medical equipment, Lavelle is criminally responsible for the botched and illegal sexual reassignment surgeries she performs, evidence of which Wendy happens upon by mistake when trying to convince the good doctor, a staunch opponent of passing, to keep her body's history a secret from her fiancé.

With 'male' and 'female' losing their denotative value in this case, even when it comes to the lab's processing of evidence, 'Ch-Ch-Changes' asks, what is normal? 'We are normal people, trying to live a normal life,' Lavelle's husband, Francis (Don McManus), shouts to the police when they search their house. 'He was a guy, he seemed normal,' the manager of the storage company tells Brass when asked to describe the person who paid for the unit where a second corpse and horrific-looking surgical equipment are discovered. 'Normal people

127

Dr Mona Lavelle aka Karl Benway and her husband Francis

don't torture people in storage bins,' Catherine retorts after hearing Brass's account and remembering the primitive equipment and bloody makeshift tools found there.

True enough. The 'normal' guy who rented the storage bin was Francis Lavelle. He killed Wendy to preserve the secret of his wife's illegal and not always successful surgeries, and with the supplementary intent of protecting their 'good' work (and future incomes). Still, Mona and Francis Lavelle look like everyone else: they live in a comfortable home with a daughter, Tippi (Savannah Ajar), born of a surrogate. Yet Dr Mona Lavelle, the psychological counsellor to the 'genitally disenfranchised', as she describes her patients, is also Dr Karl Benway, the ghostly surgeon who performs the clandestine and primitive operations inside the storage unit. Furthermore, 'Benway' is not a pseudonym but her birth name: Mona herself is a transsexual, although she has not had the surgery, presumably because of the medical establishment that 'disenfranchised' her personally as well as professionally. She still looks female in every respect (and Lindsay Crouse, who plays her, is a familiar film and TV character actress) except for her genitalia – and the fact that she still has a penis helps to sort out the last bits of misleading DNA evidence in this case. Francis, on the other hand, apparently *has* had the gender reassignment surgery. Nick presumes that, since Mona was born Karl, 'Tippi has two dads and one mom', so the surrogate has to correct him: 'Actually, it's two moms and a dad.'

Much as in 'Fur and Loathing', Grissom is the one CSI who views the constructedness of gender made evident by this case with sympathetic interest and tolerant understanding; but that is because he is a fellow 'outsider', as Mimosa (Kate Walsh), another transsexual, tells Grissom after she seeks him out to provide information that may help solve her friend Wendy's murder. By contrast, the lab rats and younger members of the CSI team as a whole seem rather skittish in their responses to what this case tells them about the instability of gender, theirs not excepted; they are unnerved by the evidence and react defensively to preserve their normative understanding of 'male' and

The transsexual Mimosa talks with fellow outsider Grissom

'female', which this episode challenges. Greg, for instance, marches into Grissom's office and declares, 'For the record I really like having a penis.' In a bar catering to transsexuals and their johns, Nick sees someone preparing to take an injection but it turns out to be silicone and not smack, as he supposed. 'Gives you good cheekbones,' he is told. Mercedes (Jazzmun), a surviving victim of Dr Lavelle's botched surgeries, teases the nervous criminalist about his mistake, saying with a straight face that 'the ones who can't buy silicone ... buy motor oil'. For a moment Nick believes her, so Mercedes reassures him: 'Calm down, pretty boy. We're not the monsters. The real freaks are the suit-and-ties who want to take a walk on the wild side – before sneaking back to the wife and kids.'

Nick is perhaps the most conventional member of the CSI team. He tries to hold on to his sense of normalcy yet be tolerant and non-judgmental. As he surveys Lady Heather's Dominion in 'Slaves of Las Vegas', Nick proudly tells Catherine, 'You know what I just realised?'

CATHERINE: Hmm?

NICK: None of this weirds me out anymore.

CATHERINE: People are just as twisted in their own living rooms. The props are different here. That's all.

NICK: Well, not everybody's twisted.

CATHERINE: Everybody, Nick. Wake up and smell the species.

NICK: Catherine, do you really think that those freaks out there, running around with their little dog collars on getting spanked, are the same as you and me?

CATHERINE: Just because you never did it doesn't mean you never could.

NICK: No way, never gonna happen.

CATHERINE: Hey, relax, Nick. All I'm saying is you're human.

NICK: Hey, man, my mom and dad are human, and—

CATHERINE: There's one thing you learn on this job is that human beings are capable of anything.

Taking a different attitude toward the weird behaviour here than in 'Fur and Loathing', Catherine insists upon open-mindedness as the benefit of their objectivity as scientists. If 'people are just as twisted

131

'None of this weirds me out anymore,' Nick says to Catherine

in their own living rooms' because 'human beings are capable of anything', then it follows that humanity ('the species') is a much larger category than normalcy ('mom and dad'), so the two are not synonymous terms; what is more, the freaks (in this case, Lady Heather, her employees, their clients) and the geeks (the criminalists) are not as far apart as Nick wants to think. In fact, Catherine and Lady Heather, both single mothers, turn out to have a lot in common. They admire each other's spirit and independence, and stand out as attractive alternatives to the powerful, castrating female attorney whose husband accidentally kills Mona Taylor.

> LADY HEATHER: Don't take this the wrong way, but I think you've got everything it takes to make a great dominatrix.
> CATHERINE: I take that as a compliment.
> LADY HEATHER: Well, you should. It's just about knowing yourself, being strong, and not taking any crap from powerful jerks who are used to giving it all day long.

More important is the connection Lady Heather makes with Grissom. At one point, from the subtlety with which she reads the power dynamics of Eileen and Cameron Nelson's marriage through their body language in a photograph, Grissom concludes that Lady Heather could join his team and work for him. She, in turn, can look him in the eye and, rather like Melanie Grace, 'see' his secret:

> LADY HEATHER: The most telling thing about anyone is what scares them. And I know what you fear more than anything, Mr Grissom.
> GRISSOM: Which is?
> LADY HEATHER: Being known. You can't accept that I might know what you really desire, because that would mean that I know you. Something, for whatever reason, you spend your entire life making sure no one else does.
> GRISSOM: Lady Heather, you're an anthropologist.
> LADY HEATHER: More tea?

Lady Heather and Grissom take tea together

Not surprisingly, Grissom evades Lady Heather's comment that he fears being known, as if intimacy were tantamount to being probed and comprehended in much the same way that the body's interior is routinely visualised on this series by the CSI shot; yet his backing away from the conversation, responding to what the statement represents rather than to what it says about him, confirms her insight. It's significant, too, that, in changing the subject, he calls Lady Heather 'an anthropologist'; although 'psychologist' would be the more apt term, since she is diagnosing his psyche, anthropology establishes their common ground as fellow ethnographers, he in his lab, she in her dominion. What is more, Lady Heather proves to be his intellectual match in this field. 'I find all deviant behaviour fascinating,' Grissom tells her in an earlier conversation, 'in that to understand our human nature we have to understand our aberrations.' She, however, challenges his terminology: 'And you think what goes on here is aberrant?' After all, she continues: 'Every job has its peculiar hazards. Rock stars damage their ear drums. Football players ruin their knees. In this business, it's scars. But no one who works for me has ever sustained a serious injury.' When Grissom counters by noting, 'Mona did – she died,' Lady Heather reminds him, 'Not because she worked here – that's your assumption.'

Lady Heather's rapport with Grissom has struck a chord with many viewers, prompting her return in three additional episodes over the years, and inspiring a great deal of fan fiction about their pairing. Her popularity was no doubt due to her being the first character to bring out fully the vexing, because complicated, question of Grissom's sexuality. Does his clumsiness with 'normal' social relations indicate a sexual void as well? He does intentionally withdraw from most human contact except when working, as Lady Heather immediately senses during their first conversation. 'It's people who don't come to places like this that I worry about,' she states after informing Grissom that her business is not about violence but fantasy, comparing it with the theatre. 'The ones who don't have an outlet. Say . . . someone like yourself.' He has outlets, he says, but they are all solitary ones: reading, riding roller-coasters, studying insects. 'And your sex life?' Lady Heather asks, to which Grissom replies with an inscrutable smile, 'It doesn't involve going to the theatre.'

Lady Heather appears to awaken Grissom's dormant sex life in 'Slaves of Las Vegas', but whether or not he then acts upon his desire when they meet again in the follow-up episode, 'Lady Heather's Box', is intentionally left ambiguous, as the DVD commentary notes. One thing is certain, though: Grissom's emotional diffidence goes hand in hand with his intellectual curiosity about all sorts of human aberrations, and this combination of qualities is what makes him a superb criminalist, the tops in his field. But it also gets in the way of his establishing relations with women who intrigue him as fellow outsiders. Lady Heather will not forgive him when he suspects she may be responsible for a murder in 'Lady Heather's Box', and Melanie Grace feels similarly hurt when he views her as a suspect in 'A Little Murder'. Such moments personalise Grissom's characterisation by enabling an audience to read it as evidence of his dysfunctionality on multiple levels – social, emotional, sexual.

What's then notable about this understanding of Grissom is that, other than his hereditary hearing loss, which was corrected by surgery in the third season finale, *CSI* has never given him a developed backstory to account for his fear of being known. In refraining from locating his dysfunctionality in a traumatic origin, the characterisation therefore resists conventional TV psychology. As I observed in an earlier chapter, the lack of strongly serialised backstory arcs for all the investigators but Catherine reflects the imperative, often voiced by Grissom, that the investigators not become personally involved in a case. Additionally, it stabilises the CSIs' characterisations so that, serving the purposes of the series's narrative premise of forensic investigations, the team members do not vary that much from season to season. (The most noticeable changes, in fact, involve Catherine's hairstyles each year or whether Grissom does or does not sport a beard.) Grissom's individuating features – his brilliance, his learnedness, his curiosity, his solitariness, his social awkwardness with people, his many eccentricities – remain simply that, a set of qualities that suit (in the double sense of typifying and enabling) his profession as a scientist. In this regard, the series too can be called anthropological more than psychological not only in how it understands human behaviour through Grissom, but in how it views the man himself, accepting him on his own terms, so to speak.

135

For this reason, if the lab *is* the centre of the world as far as *CSI* is concerned, and it surely is so, then Grissom is not dysfunctional at all. Everyone in the lab not only respects him but seeks his approval, too. As well as being a brilliant if eccentric scientist who serves as his team's inspiring leader, Grissom mentors his younger colleagues. In teaching them how to be better criminalists, he encourages them to appreciate difference – to find all deviant behaviour fascinating – and to do so from the outsider's perspective. Thus late in 'A Little Murder', Nick and Sara repeat what Grissom has earlier said in their presence about the little people's need to adapt to the world when it won't adapt to them; not surprisingly, it is recalling his mentor's comment that leads Nick to the case's solution. Likewise, in 'Slaves of Las Vegas' and 'Ch-Ch-Changes', Nick tries to emulate Grissom in not being judgmental, although, as already indicated, the disciple is not yet the equal of his teacher.

With the exception of Catherine and Brass, who are treated as Grissom's peers in terms of experience and authority, the entire CSI team, along with the various lab technicians, can be considered wannabe Grissoms – an assortment of geeky social misfits driven more by the intellectual puzzles presented by a crime scene than by their personal demons. The attention to their professionalism keeps each episode firmly grounded on the strange case or cases of the moment, but it also characterises them all as workaholics; when referred to in throwaway dialogue, their private lives are revealed to be problematic, non-existent or just irrelevant. Indeed, the few times a team member is made the protagonist in a case – when Catherine's ex-husband dies and her daughter almost drowns ('Lady Heather's Box'), or she is tricked into thinking she has been date-raped ('Built to Kill, Parts One and Two'); when Nick becomes involved with a former suspect in a case and is then suspected of her murder ('Boom'), or he is buried underground ('Grave Danger'); when Brass is almost fatally injured when negotiating a hostage situation ('Bang-Bang' and 'Way to Go'); when Greg tries to save a man from a mob beating ('Fannysmackin''); when Sara is abducted by the miniature killer and left to die in the desert ('Living Doll' and 'Dead Doll'); when Warrick is drugged and framed for a murder and then, once vindicated, shot by the corrupt undersheriff ('For Gedda') – she or he is subjected to sadistic violence. It makes one wonder if a CSI's unusual story prominence in an episode requires, as a kind of compensation or even comeuppance for taking centre stage in a case, prolonged, not to say excessive, pain and suffering.

At most other times, character backstory is kept to a minimum, even when, at least according to the conventions of television drama, it ought to be more fully dramatised (as happens, for instance, on the two CSI spin-offs, which sustain more developed story arcs for their leads). To be sure, CSI is not the only TV crime show that treats its regular characters this way. During its nearly twenty years on the air, Law and Order has paid little attention to the personal lives of its

136

regular characters except when writing them off the show. But one is always more cognisant of the minimalism of *CSI* when it incorporates what for another series would be ample material for a strong story arc involving the regular characters. For instance, following the 100th episode, in 'Mea Culpa' Ecklie broke up the team, assigning Nick and Warrick to the swing shift with Catherine promoted as their supervisor. After several episodes, the team's reunion was prompted by a single line of dialogue toward the end of 'Grave Danger'. 'I want my guys back,' Grissom tells Ecklie. Despite spoilers on the Internet that predicted Catherine's return to the graveyard shift would generate conflict for her between career ambition and loyalty to her colleagues, once the group is reunited in 'Bodies in Motion', the impact of her demotion was ignored. 'So you get the team back together only to break us apart again?' she asks Grissom from the field when he assigns Warrick and her a case by mobile telephone – and that's how we learn that Ecklie's division of the team has been undone after 'Grave Danger'.

Judging from the strong fan interest in the CSI team on the Internet as well as the series's high ratings, the incomplete backstories do not impede identification but foster it, whether by eliciting intrigue (because characters are somewhat enigmatic) or inviting participation on the viewers' part (to fill in the gaps).[62] For me, the lack of fully dramatised backstories beyond their professional lives connects the CSIs to the people they investigate; if only because of their intellect and training, the CSIs also remain somewhat out of sync with normalcy in so far as they are defined by the work they do and the talents they bring to it, and not by their personal relationships.

So in talking about the indeterminate or condensed characterisation of the CSIs, I do not mean to suggest that they are simply ciphers or stick figures. Grissom's characterisation as an impartial, distanced and in his own way freakish observer of human behaviour is nicely captured in a conversation that occurs toward the end of 'The Hunger Artist'. The scientist walks alongside Cassie James (Susan Misner), Ashleigh's sister and a former fashion model herself who, suffering from schizophrenic paranoia, has become a bag lady.

(Befitting this conversation, too, immediately afterwards Grissom will learn from his doctor that, without surgery, his hereditary hearing loss may become irreparable.)

> GRISSOM: Would you like me to help you get in a shelter?
> CASSIE: No, I would need a shelter from a shelter. No, no, no. Out here, I can hunt and I can range and I can find the things that I need out here. I mean, you never know what you need until you find it.
> GRISSOM: Or until you lose it.
> CASSIE: I mean, all we are is what we try to get rid of. Fat and newspapers and loneliness and cat food cans. And there are going-away people and there are left-behind people but, you know, everybody's secrets . . . everybody's secrets are the same.
> GRISSOM: Were your and your sister's secrets the same?
> CASSIE: My sister didn't have secrets. Her secrets had her. That . . . I told you I didn't . . . I don't know. I mean, you know, y-y-you, you can pick through a million lives and never have one of your own.

Grissom walks with Cassie James at the end of 'The Hunger Artist'

GRISSOM: Looking for things, analysing them . . . trying to figure out the world – that's a life.

The dialogue shows Grissom's sympathetic concern for Cassie because of her mental illness and his appreciation of her independence, while underlining their fellowship as outsiders: not only are both isolated from the normal world because of their respective impairments but, in a telling comparison of his profession with her homelessness, both spend their days picking through the world's garbage and uncovering its secrets. When Grissom utters his last line about 'looking for things, analysing them', meant to console Cassie's sense of her non-being, he is just as clearly offering a justification of his own life as a scientist and as an outsider: 'trying to figure out the world – that's a life'. That outsider's perspective, when all is said and done, is what holds my interest in the cases as they are investigated. It's why I still look forward to new episodes of *CSI* and why I still take pleasure from the reruns.

Afterword

Any serious viewer of *CSI* will know that what I was pointing out about Grissom in the previous chapter seemed to change course at the very end of season six. The coda of 'Way to Go' disclosed that he and Sara Sidle are having a clandestine love affair. This revelation took most viewers by surprise and was well covered by the entertainment press, because, as often pointed out in the DVD commentaries, beginning with her arrival in the second episode, the series had deliberately established that, while she was infatuated with Grissom, he had feelings for her but could not articulate just what they were. At least until that coda, their private interactions in the lab were always ambiguously scripted; overlaid with conflicting possibilities, their scenes together repeatedly dramatised Grissom's inability to move one way or the other.

The abruptness of the episode's big reveal was consistent with the lack of developed backstories for the characters on *CSI*. How or when the Grissom–Sara relationship had got past the stalemate of the past six years was not recounted. Yes, one could infer that Grissom decided to take action after Brass nearly died in 'Way to Go', but there were also indications, some planted in post-season interviews with William Petersen, Jorja Fox and show runner Carol Mendelsohn, that the relationship may well have been consummated before this episode. Many fans on Internet chat boards therefore began reviewing earlier episodes of the sixth season in search of telltale clues and then looked back to previous seasons for additional clues. The coda, moreover, thrilled those viewers who had been rooting for a Grissom–Sara pairing all along, but turned off just as many others, with a large contingent preferring Lady Heather as a more suitable consort for Grissom.

I suspect that the sudden disclosure of a Grissom–Sara sexual relationship in a cliffhanger of sorts was a ratings ploy that had a lot to do with ABC's decision to move its popular medical soap opera *Grey's Anatomy* opposite *CSI* for the new season to follow. This schedule change was officially announced at around the time 'Way to Go' aired, but rumours of ABC's plan had gone public before then. Nonetheless, Mendelsohn insisted after the season six finale's big surprise, and with reference to the future competition from *Grey's Anatomy* on Thursday nights, that *CSI* would not change: 'We are not a soap opera. We are not a serial.'[63]

As a couple, Grissom and Sara thankfully remained at the margins of episodes after viewers were let in on their secret. Reduced mainly to knowing looks while together at work, their relationship was finally revealed to their colleagues only when, as the latest victim of the miniature killer, Sara was left to die in the desert in the season seven finale. (She would subsequently be rescued in the opening of season eight.) Before then, what little we saw of their intimacy when they were not working seemed to me generically manufactured, starting with the inclusion of Grissom's home life. In 'Leapin' Lizards', a scene of Grissom and Sara watching TV in bed and eating yogurt disclosed that he owned a dog, a Boxer mix. The dog was there to give Grissom a reason to leave Sara alone for several minutes; when he took the animal outside for a walk, she found an unmailed love letter he had written to her while on a month's sabbatical back East.

The dog's presence stood out as a clumsy plot device in a conventional domestic scene meant to signify 'intimacy' for the couple. After all, that dog was nowhere to be seen in an earlier episode that had shown Grissom at home. In 'The Strip Strangler', the first season finale, Grissom is ordered to take a two-week vacation for refusing to follow the sheriff's orders. Once he is alone in his private space, classical music relaxes him, along with some prescription medicine to dull the pain of a

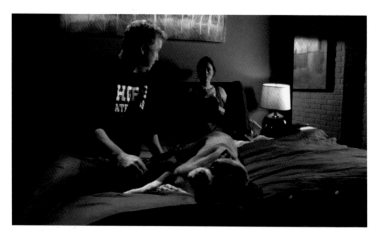

Grissom and Hank the dog with Sara

migraine. As a show of support, his team then unexpectedly appears at his home to continue working the case with him.

142

In any event, for a series that is ordinarily very consistent in the writing of the regular characters regardless of who has authored a particular script, a big, lumbering, healthy-looking mutt is an incongruous pet for Grissom to own. Not only does he spend most of his waking hours at work but Grissom has mainly shown an interest in insects, professionally and recreationally. Grissom, viewers already knew from season two's 'Ellie', races cockroaches for sport ('hissing roaches from Madagascar', actually). And to make his ownership of a dog seem even more arbitrary, in subsequent episodes of seasons seven and eight this pet acquired a name, 'Hank'. Apparently no one – whether in the fictive world or the writers' room – seemed to recall that, during seasons two and three, Sara had been dating Hank Peddigrew (Christopher Wiehl), an emergency service driver who was secretly involved with another woman at the same time. A simple coincidence? Perhaps. Or was there some intent, be it innocent or devious, on Grissom's part when he chose the name of Sara's cheating ex-lover for his dog? Maybe, but not as likely. Or did Grissom's relation with Sara force the writers to engage in a bit of retconning (as fans of serial fiction shorten the idea of 'retroactive continuity') in order to construct a private life for him? Based on the evidence, that's my theory.

The false note sounded by Hank the dog is symptomatic of how the handling of Grissom's relationship with Sara has had the effect of making him seem, well, commonplace. Their scenes together as a couple seem to be written without much imagination or conviction, in no small way because the effect of this relationship has been to normalise him, to turn him into more of 'a regular guy' – that is, a middle-aged professional with a girlfriend, a dog and a condominium in which to eat yogurt in bed while watching TV – just like many of CSI's viewers and CBS's main demographic.

Time will tell if CSI jumped the shark with Grissom and Sara. While Grissom's private life did not intrude upon any of the investigations, and so from this perspective his relationship with Sara has had a negligible impact on CSI overall, the decision to move him in that direction nonetheless has heightened my impression that the series has gradually been softening its edginess. Lady Heather, for instance, returned in seasons six ('Pirates of the Third Reich') and seven ('The Good, the Bad and the Dominatrix') but her story function in both episodes was that of a mother grieving for her daughter, which significantly domesticated the more radical persona of the character as first introduced in 'Slaves of Las Vegas'.

The eighth season also indicates an uncertain future for the series, because it marked the departure of two of its regulars, breaking up the original cast for the first time. Due to Jorja Fox's exit from the show, in 'Goodbye and Good Luck' Sara left her job and Las Vegas but not yet the relationship with Grissom, which continued to be referenced in subsequent episodes. Additionally, Gary Dourdan's character Warrick was shot in the neck at close range in the season closer, 'For Gedda' – and since it was announced before that episode aired that this actor would be leaving the series too, the wound appeared to be fatal.

CSI will survive the loss of those two characters but what about Grissom? In the past, William Petersen has publicly carped about the network's cloning of *CSI* with the 'Miami' and 'New York' spin-offs, and his eventual departure has been anticipated since season seven, when he arranged to take a sabbatical in mid-season in order to do live theatre. The renewal of his contract for an additional year was announced shortly after 'For Gedda' aired, and this information was released in order to reassure nervous fans about the series's future when Dourdan's exit came so soon after Fox's. However, it was confirmed some time later that the ninth season would not only be Petersen's last as a regular cast member but that he would leave after the tenth episode (and then continue to serve off camera as one of the show's numerous executive producers).[64]

Can there be a *CSI* without Gil Grissom? Obviously, as Petersen's temporary replacement by Liev Schreiber (playing Michael Keppler, a character designed to be the opposite of Grissom in every way) indicated in season seven, the format can accommodate new characters. In fact, the disclosure of Petersen's exit from the series after only ten more episodes was accompanied by further announcement of several planned additions to the cast, including a new figure imagined as Grissom's successor. Yet I doubt if *CSI* will be the same show without Grissom's singular perspective on a case or his style as a team leader, in clear contrast to the more conventional leadership roles of his counterparts in 'Miami' and 'New York' (and indeed of Schreiber's character during his brief incumbency, too).

Whatever the future holds for *CSI* once Petersen departs, though, the series's achievements in reinvigorating the crime show genre will not be disputed, whether emphasis is placed on its representation of science, its thrilling visual style or its understanding of Vegas culture. In dramatising forensic investigation as an intellectual activity, *CSI* has made it seem fascinating enough to engage the interest of millions of viewers week after week for eight seasons running, and that is no mean accomplishment.

Notes

Quotations of dialogue from episides of *CSI* are my transcriptions from the CBS-Paramount DVD sets as double-checked against the transcripts for the series archived at the *CSI* section at Twiz TV.com <www.twiztv.com/scripts/csi>.

1 Josef Adalian, 'Star Appeal High on Eye's Web List: CBS Plans to be "Survivor" of Fall Season with New Demo Group', *Daily Variety* (6 September 2000): <www.variety.com>, downloaded 16 April 2006.

2 Ray Richmond, untitled interview with Anthony Zuiker, Ann Donahue, Carol Mendelsohn and Danny Cannon on the occasion of *CSI*'s 100th episode, *The Hollywood Reporter* (18 November 2004), downloaded from LexisNexis 28 February 2008; and Rebecca Weiss, 'The Cornell Connection: Carol Mendelsohn '73', *The Cornell Daily Sun* online (27 November 2007): <www.cornellsun.com>, downloaded 5 December 2007.

3 Michael Schneider and Josef Adalian, 'Eye's Maple-Leaf Alliance: Canuck Producer Recruited to "C.S.I." Team', *Daily Variety* (9 August 2000): <www.variety.com>, downloaded 16 April 2006.

4 Josef Adalian, 'Touchstone Seeking Exit from Eye Deal: Studio Wants Out of CBS Actioner "C.S.I." ', *Daily Variety* (23 June 2000): <www.variety.com>, downloaded 16 April 2006.

5 Rick Kissell and Josef Adalian, 'Eye's Wow Bows Power Weekend: "Fugitive" Unspectacular Given Big Promo Push', *Daily Variety* (9 October 2000): <www.variety.com>, downloaded 16 April 2006.

6 Steve Clarke, 'UK's Five Sells "CSI Miami" via VOD: Web Inks Deal with BT and Alliance Atlantis', *Daily Variety* (13 October 2006): <www.variety.com>, downloaded 13 October 2006. For a view of the series that examines it from the standpoint of its commercial function as an imported programme on British television, see Simone Knox, 'Five's Finest: The Import of *CSI* to British Terrestrial Television', in Michael Allen (ed.), *Reading CSI: Crime TV under the Microscope* (London: I. B. Taurus, 2007), pp. 183–97.

7 Magz Osborne, 'Yanks Fuel Sony's Asian Paybox: "Survivor," "Fear," "24" Boost AXN Ratings', *Variety* (17 August 2005): <www.variety.com>, downloaded 11 October 2006.

8 Elizabeth Guider, ' "CSI" Registers Strong O'Seas Sales: Bruckheimer Hits Mipcom to Tout Skein', *Daily Variety* (4 October 2000): <www.variety.com>, downloaded 25 June 2007.

9 Marisse Strauss, 'AAC Smash CSI Celebrates 300 Eps', *Playback* (16 October 2006): <www.playbackmag.com>, downloaded 17 October 2006.

10 Rick Kissell, 'Eye's "CSI" Joins Elite Club: CBS Drama Surpassed 25 Million Viewers During Sweeps', *Daily Variety* (11 December 2001): <www.variety.com>, downloaded 16 April 2006.

11 Tom R. Tyler, 'Viewing *CSI* and the Threshold of Guilt: Managing Truth and Justice in Reality and Fiction', *Yale Law Journal* vol. 115 no. 5 (2006), p. 1065.

12 According to Rick Workman, a real-life criminalist in southern Nevada, protocols regarding the status of CSIs vary across the

Greater Las Vegas area, depending on the municipality. In Vegas proper, the criminalists are not members of the police force, but they have the option to carry guns. In neighbouring North Las Vegas, they are a mix of civilian and police, and in suburban Henderson, they are civilians but police also process crime scenes. Elsewhere in Nevada, Boulder City detectives function doubly, collecting evidence in their capacity as criminalists while interviewing or arresting in their other capacity as police; and Reno CSIs are sworn deputies with full police powers. Workman concludes, 'There are thousands of different combinations of these scenarios throughout the US, and even more throughout the world.' Rick Workman, 'The CSI Effect', in Donn Cortez with Leah Wilson (eds), *Investigating* CSI: *An Unauthorized Look Inside the Crime Labs of Las Vegas, Miami, and New York* (Dallas, TX: BenBella Books, 2006), p. 32.

146

13 Danny Cannon, a frequent director and writer of *CSI*, recalls that the pilot was not planned as 'a cop show', so it deliberately 'didn't have macho guys chasing after each other and having all the answers'. However, the pilot, which aired as the first episode, followed the hierarchy of the real-life Las Vegas forensic unit in having a high-ranking police officer, Detective Brass, head the fictionalised version. In order to make the unity of the CSI team more pronounced as a group separated from the police force, the second episode, 'Cool Change', reassigned Brass to Homicide and put Grissom in charge. Mike Flaherty, *CSI: Crime Scene Investigation Companion* (New York: Pocket Books, 2004), pp. 15, 18.

14 The one newsworthy exception was when Jorja Fox and George Eads, holding out for a large salary increase, were fired by CBS in July 2004 for failing to report to the set at the start of season five. After some

negotiating with the network, the actors returned to work under the terms of their existing contracts.

15 Laura Moore, 'CSI Stars Spend a Night at the Museum', *TV Guide* (24 May 2007): <www.tvguide.com>, downloaded 24 May 2007.

16 For a comparison of CSI protocols on TV and in real-life cases in Seattle, Washington, see Kira Millage, 'CSI: Fact and Fiction', *The Bellingham Herald* (22 March 2006): <www.news/ bellinghamherald.com>, downloaded 25 March 2006.

17 Workman, 'The CSI Effect', p. 29.

18 Ibid., pp. 31–2.

19 Tyler, 'Viewing *CSI* and the Threshold of Guilt', p. 1053. See also Simon Cole and Rachel Dissoso, 'Law and the Lab', *Wall Street Journal* (13 May 2005): <www.truthinjustice.org/law-lab.htem>, downloaded 10 June 2007.

20 Tyler, 'Viewing *CSI*', p. 1063.

21 Michael D. Mann, 'The CSI Effect: Better Jurors through Television and Science?', *Buffalo Public Interest Law Journal* vol. 24 (2005–6), p. 161.

22 Tyler, 'Viewing *CSI*', p. 1063.

23 Jeffrey Toobin, 'The CSI Effect: The Truth about Forensic Science', *New Yorker* (7 May 2007), pp. 31, 33.

24 Mann, 'The CSI Effect', p. 180.

25 Ibid., pp. 178–9.

26 Toobin, 'The CSI Effect', p. 31.

27 The music soundtrack and sound are also significant stylistic elements, but this book's length limitations, as well as my own inclination toward the visual over the aural, dictate my concentration solely on the series's look. But see Karen Lury, '*CSI* and Sound', in Allen (ed.), *Reading* CSI, pp. 107–21.

28 'CSI 100th: The Minds behind the Bodies', *Hollywood Reporter* (18 November

2004), downloaded from lexisnexis.com, 28 February 2008.

29 Flaherty, *CSI*, p. 15.

30 Deborah Jermyn, 'Body Matters: Realism and the Corpse in *CSI*', in Allen (ed.), *Reading* CSI, p. 80.

31 Richmond, interview with Zuiker *et al.*

32 Jermyn, 'Body Matters', p. 80; Martha Gever, 'The Spectacle of Crime, Digitized: *CSI: Crime Scene Investigation* and Social Anatomy', *European Journal of Cultural Studies* vol. 8 no. 4 (2005), p. 457.

33 Marita Sturken and Lisa Cartwright, *Practices of Looking: An Introduction to Visual Culture* (New York: Oxford University Press, 2001), pp. 281, 286.

34 Gever, 'Spectacle of Crime', p. 460.

35 Ibid., p. 456.

36 Elke Weissman and Karen Boyle, 'Evidence of Things Unseen: The Pornographic Aesthetic and the Search for Truth in *CSI*', in Allen (ed.), *Reading* CSI, p. 97.

37 Janine Hiddlestone, 'All that Glitters: Coloring Place and Identity in *CSI*', in Cortez with Wilson (eds), *Investigating CSI*, pp. 162–3, 166–7.

38 'The CSI Tour', season three DVD supplement, disc six.

39 Silke Panse, ' "The Bullets Confirm the Story Told by the Potato": Materials without Motives in *CSI: Crime Scene Investigation*', in Allen (ed.), *Reading* CSI, p. 154.

40 Flaherty, *CSI*, p. 15.

41 Michael Schneider, 'Widescreen Television: Bruckheimer's Big-Picture Values Made "Feature TV" a Natural Fit', *Daily Variety* (9 July 2006): <www.variety.com>, downloaded 14 July 2006.

42 Strauss, 'AAC Smash'.

43 Flaherty, *CSI*, p. 15.

44 'The New Title Sequence', *CSI: Crime Scene Investigation*, season six DVD supplement, disc six.

45 For a case-study of a single episode's production, in this case 'Suckers', see 'The Evolution of an Episode from Concept to Completion', season four DVD supplement, disc six.

46 Weissman and Boyle, 'Evidence of Things Unseen', p. 97.

47 David Wiener, 'Hot on the Trail: Directors of Photography Jonathan West, ASC and Michael Barrett Illuminate Clues for the Series "C.S.I.: Crime Scene Investigation" ', *American Cinematographer* vol. 83 no. 3 (March 2002), p. 63.

48 Douglas Bankston, 'Searching for Clues', *American Cinematographer* vol. 82 no. 5 (May 2001), pp. 58–60, 62–5.

49 Jack Tirak, 'The Tiffany Network Sparkles in High Definition' (21 July 2006), Erie Media-Go-Round: <www.eriemedia.blogspot.com>, downloaded 27 July 2007. CBS and Paramount Home Video, moreover, made a mistake when issuing the first season of *CSI* on DVD, since they did not format it in enhanced widescreen, causing a consumer outcry; that misstep was corrected in all successive season releases.

50 Both HDMI and component connections transmit the richest colour on video. HDMI, like its forerunner DVI, is a digital-based feed via a single cable from a video source (high-definition cable or DVD), so it delivers the three separate colours directly through a bitstream. Component is analogue-based; it requires three RCA-type cables, usually coloured green, blue and red, and it sends a separated colour feed to its target by transmitting the luminescence (or total brightness) of the image through the green cable, and subtracting the red and blue values from the luminescence signal for independent transmission through the two other connections. Another key difference is that component, the connection of choice

147

for DVD players, works on standard as well as high-definition equipment, whereas HDMI is exclusively high-definition. In addition, unlike component or even DVI, HDMI transmits sound as well as the picture. For a simple explanation aimed at a lay person, see the useful article, 'DVI and HDMI Versus Component Video – Which is Better?' at Blue Jeans Cable, a commercial site: <www.bluejeanscable.com/articles/dvihdmicomponent.htm>, downloaded 27 July 2007.

51 Karen Lury, *Interpreting Television* (London: Hodder Arnold, 2005), pp. 56, 46, 50.

52 Gever, 'Spectacle of Crime', p. 458.

53 Lury, *Interpreting Television*, p. 47.

54 William L. Fox, *In the Desert of Desire: Las Vegas and the Culture of Spectacle* (Reno: University of Nevada Press, 2005).

55 For background on the history of Las Vegas, to which I am indebted for the information I include in this chapter, see Fox, *In the Desert of Desire*; Barbara Land and Myrick Land, *A Short History of Las Vegas*, 2nd edn. (Reno: University of Nevada Press, 2004); Hal Rothman, *Neon Metropolis: How Las Vegas Started the Twenty-First Century* (New York: Routledge, 2003); Geoff Schumacher, *Sun, Sin & Suburbia: An Essential History of Las Vegas* (Las Vegas: Stephens Press LCC, 2004).

56 For a brief account of the Vegas period of Hughes's life and of the development of Summerlin, see Schumacher, *Sun, Sin & Suburbia*, pp. 96–133.

57 Except for Area 51, *CSI* also makes little mention of the long-standing presence of

the military and nuclear testing in the desert, which further contributes to and economically amplifies the history of 'old' and even 'new' Vegas. Nuclear testing, in fact, was a major factor in Hughes's abrupt departure from the Desert Inn and it did not cease entirely until the early 1990s. See Rothman, *Neon Metropolis*, p. 131.

58 Fox, *In the Desert of Desire*, p. xi.

59 Ibid., p. 29.

60 Ibid., p. xii.

61 Rothman, *Neon Metropolis*, p. 63

62 At the *CSI* Wiki <www.csi.wetpaint.com>, the section devoted to 'characters' has pages for each that collates every bit of personal information, scattered across episodes often cryptically during the years, into a coherently narrated backstory, along with lists of defining episodes, significant relationships and personal trivia. Another fan site of note, by the way, is The *CSI* Files <csifiles.com>, which collates daily news stories, features, spoilers and interviews related to any of the three series in the franchise. Both websites also feature discussion boards.

63 Maureen Ryan, 'Solving the Mystery of the "CSI" Finale Shocker', *Chicago Tribune* online, 25 May 2006, downloaded 28 May 2006.

64 Michael Ausiello, 'William Petersen Says B-Y-E to *CSI*', *Entertainment Weekly*, 25 July 2008, p. 60; and 'William Petersen Exits "CSI": Actor to Remain Exec Producer on CBS Show', *Daily Variety* (16 July 2008): <www.variety.com>, downloaded 16 July 2008.

Credits

CSI:
Crime Scene Investigation

USA/2000

Created by Anthony E. Zuiker

regular cast
William Petersen (Gil Grissom)
Marg Helgenberger (Catherine Willows)
Gary Dourdan (Warrick Brown)
George Eads (Nick Stokes)
Jorja Fox (Sara Sidle)
Eric Szmanda (Greg Sanders)
Robert David Hall (Dr Al Robbins)
Paul Guilfoyle (Captain Jim Brass)
David Berman (David Phillips)
Wallace Langham (David Hodges)

© CBS Worldwide Inc. and Alliance Atlantis Productions, Inc.
Production Companies
Jerry Bruckheimer Films [later Jerry Bruckheimer Television]/Alliance Atlantis/CBS Productions

Season 1
1.1 *Pilot*
(tx 6 October 2000)
dir. Danny Cannon, wr. Anthony E. Zuiker
1.2 *Cool Change*
(tx 13 October 2000)
dir. Michael W. Watkins, wr. Anthony E. Zuiker
1.3 *Crate 'n' Burial*
(tx 20 October 2000)
dir. Danny Cannon, wr. Ann Donahue
1.4 *Pledging Mr Johnson*
(tx 27 October 2000)
dir. Richard J. Lewis, wr. Josh Berman, Anthony E. Zuiker

1.5 *Friends & Lovers*
(tx 3 November 2000)
dir. Lou Antonio, wr. Andrew Lipsitz
1.6 *Who Are You?*
(tx 10 November 2000)
dir. Danny Cannon, wr. Carol Mendelsohn, Josh Berman
1.7 *Blood Drops*
(tx 17 November 2000)
dir. Kenneth Fink, tele. Ann Donahue, st. Tish McCarthy
1.8 *Anonymous*
(tx 24 November 2000)
dir. Danny Cannon, wr. Eli Talbert, Anthony E. Zuiker
1.9 *Unfriendly Skies*
(tx 8 December 2000)
dir. Michael Shapiro, tele. Andrew Lipsitz, Carol Mendelsohn, Anthony E. Zuiker, st. Andrew Lipsitz
1.10 *Sex, Lies and Larvae*
(tx 22 December 2000)
dir. Thomas J. Wright, wr. Josh Berman, Ann Donahue
1.11 *I-15 Murders*
(tx 12 January 2001)
dir. Oz Scott, wr. Carol Mendelsohn
1.12 *Fahrenheit 932*
(tx 1 February 2001)
dir. Danny Cannon, wr. Jacqueline Zambrano
1.13 *Boom*
(tx 8 February 2001)
dir. Kenneth Fink, wr. Josh Berman, Ann Donahue, Carol Mendelsohn
1.14 *To Halve and to Hold*
(tx 15 February 2001)
dir. Lou Antonio, wr. Andrew Lipsitz, Ann Donahue
1.15 *Table Stakes*
(tx 22 February 2001)
dir. Danny Cannon, tele. Anthony E. Zuiker, Carol Mendelsohn, st. Elizabeth Devine

1.16 *Too Tough to Die*
(tx 1 March 2001)
dir. Richard J. Lewis, wr. Elizabeth Devine
1.17 *Face Lift*
(tx 8 March 2001)
dir. Lou Antonio, wr. Josh Berman
1.18 *$35K O.B.O.*
(tx 29 March 2001)
dir. Roy H. Wagner, wr. Eli Talbert
1.19 *Gentle, Gentle*
(tx 12 April 2001)
dir. Danny Cannon, wr. Ann Donahue
1.20 *Sounds of Silence*
(tx 19 April 2001)
dir. Peter Markle, wr. Josh Berman, Andrew Lipsitz
1.21 *Justice Is Served*
(tx 26 April 2001)
dir. Thomas J. Wright, wr. Jerry Stahl
1.22 *Evaluation Day*
(tx 10 May 2001)
dir. Kenneth Fink, wr. Anthony E. Zuiker
1.23 *The Strip Strangler*
(tx 17 May 2001)
dir. Danny Cannon, wr. Ann Donahue

Season 2
2.1 *Burked*
(tx 27 September 2001)
dir. Danny Cannon, wr. Carol Mendelsohn, Anthony E. Zuiker
2.2 *Chaos Theory*
(tx 4 October 2001)
dir. Kenneth Fink, wr. Eli Talbert, Josh Berman
2.3 *Overload*
(tx 11 October 2001)
dir. Richard J. Lewis, wr. Josh Berman

2.4 *Bully for You*
(tx 18 October 2001)
dir. Thomas J. Wright, wr. Ann
Donahue
2.5 *Scuba Doobie-Doo*
(tx 25 October 2001)
dir. Jefery Levy, wr. Andrew
Lipsitz, Elizabeth Devine
2.6 *Alter Boys*
(tx 1 November 2001)
dir. Danny Cannon, wr. Ann
Donahue
2.7 *Caged*
(tx 8 November 2001)
dir. Richard J. Lewis,
wr. Elizabeth Devine, Carol
Mendelsohn
2.8 *Slaves of Las Vegas*
(tx 15 November 2001)
dir. Peter Markle, wr. Jerry
Stahl
2.9 *And Then There Were None*
(tx 22 November 2001)
dir. John Patterson, tele. Eli
Talbert, Carol Mendelsohn,
st. Josh Berman
2.10 *Ellie*
(tx 6 December 2001)
dir. Charles Correll,
wr. Anthony E. Zuiker
2.11 *Organ Grinder*
(tx 13 December 2001)
dir. Allison Liddi, wr. Ann
Donahue, Elizabeth Devine
2.12 *You've Got Male*
(tx 20 December 2001)
dir. Charles Correll, wr. Marc
Dube, Corey Miller
2.13 *Identity Crisis*
(tx 17 January 2002)
dir. Kenneth Fink, wr. Anthony
E. Zuiker, Ann Donahue
2.14 *The Finger*
(tx 31 January 2002)
dir. Richard J. Lewis,
wr. Danny Cannon, Carol
Mendelsohn
2.15 *Burden of Proof*
(tx 7 February 2002)
dir. Kenneth Fink, wr. Ann
Donahue
2.16 *Primum Non Nocere*
(tx 28 February 2002)
dir. Danny Cannon, wr. Andrew
Lipsitz

2.17 *Felonious Monk*
(tx 7 March 2002)
dir. Kenneth Fink, wr. Jerry
Stahl
2.18 *Chasing the Bus*
(tx 28 March 2002)
dir. Richard J. Lewis, wr. Eli
Talbert
2.19 *Stalker*
(tx 4 April 2002)
dir. Peter Markle, wr. Anthony
E. Zuiker, Danny Cannon
2.20 *Cats in the Cradle . . .*
(tx 25 April 2002)
dir. Richard J. Lewis, wr. Kristy
Dobkin
2.21 *Anatomy of a Lye*
(tx 2 May 2002)
dir. Kenneth Fink, wr. Josh
Berman, Andrew Lipsitz
2.22 *Cross-Jurisdictions*
(tx 9 May 2002)
dir. Danny Cannon,
wr. Anthony E. Zuiker, Ann
Donahue, Carol Mendelsohn
2.23 *The Hunger Artist*
(tx 18 May 2002)
dir. Richard J. Lewis, wr. Jerry
Stahl

Season 3
3.1 *Revenge Is Best Served
Cold*
(tx 26 September 2002)
dir. Danny Cannon,
wr. Anthony E. Zuiker, Carol
Mendelsohn
3.2 *The Accused Is Entitled*
(tx 3 October 2002)
dir. Kenneth Fink, wr. Ann
Donahue, Elizabeth Devine
3.3 *Let the Seller Beware*
(tx 10 October 2002)
dir. Richard J. Lewis,
wr. Andrew Lipsitz, Anthony E.
Zuiker
3.4 *A Little Murder*
(tx 17 October 2002)
dir. Tucker Gates, wr. Naren
Shankar, Ann Donahue
3.5 *Abra-Cadaver*
(tx 31 October 2002)
dir. Danny Cannon, wr. Anthony
E. Zuiker, Danny Cannon

3.6 *The Execution of Catherine
Willows*
(tx 7 November 2002)
dir. Kenneth Fink, wr. Carol
Mendelsohn, Elizabeth
Devine
3.7 *Fight Night*
(tx 14 November 2002)
dir. Richard J. Lewis,
wr. Andrew Lipsitz, Naren
Shankar
3.8 *Snuff*
(tx 21 November 2002)
dir. Kenneth Fink, wr. Ann
Donahue, Bob Harris
3.9 *Blood Lust*
(tx 5 December 2002)
dir. Charles Correll,
wr. Josh Berman, Carol
Mendelsohn
3.10 *High and Low*
(tx 12 December 2002)
dir. Richard J. Lewis,
wr. Eli Talbert, Naren Shankar
3.11 *Recipe for Murder*
(tx 9 January 2003)
dir. Richard J. Lewis, J. Miller
Tobin, wr. Anthony E. Zuiker,
Ann Donahue
3.12 *Got Murder?*
(tx 16 January 2003)
dir. Kenneth Fink, wr. Sarah
Goldfinger
3.13 *Random Acts of Violence*
(tx 30 January 2003)
dir. Danny Cannon, wr. Danny
Cannon, Naren Shankar
3.14 *One Hit Wonder*
(tx 6 February 2003)
dir. Félix Enríquez Alcalá,
wr. Corey D. Miller
3.15 *Lady Heather's Box*
(tx 13 February 2003)
dir. Richard J. Lewis,
tele. Carol Mendelsohn,
Andrew Lipsitz, Naren
Shankar, Eli Talbert,
st. Anthony E. Zuiker,
Ann Donahue, Josh Berman,
Bob Harris
3.16 *Lucky Strike*
(tx 20 February 2003)
dir. Kenneth Fink,
wr. Eli Talbert, Anthony E.
Zuiker

3.17 *Crash and Burn*
(tx 13 March 2003)
dir. Richard J. Lewis, wr. Josh Berman
3.18 *Precious Metal*
(tx 3 April 2003)
dir. Deran Sarafian, wr. Naren Shankar, Andrew Lipsitz
3.19 *A Night at the Movies*
(tx 10 April 2003)
dir. Matt Earl Beesley, tele. Danny Cannon, Anthony E. Zuiker, st. Carol Mendelsohn
3.20 *Last Laugh*
(tx 24 April 2003)
dir. Richard J. Lewis, tele. Bob Harris, Anthony E. Zuiker, st. Bob Harris, Carol Mendelsohn
3.21 *Forever*
(tx 1 May 2003)
dir. David Grossman, wr. Sarah Goldfinger
3.22 *Play with Fire*
(tx 8 May 2003)
dir. Kenneth Fink, wr. Naren Shankar, Andrew Lipsitz
3.23 *Inside the Box*
(tx 15 May 2003)
dir. Danny Cannon, wr. Carol Mendelsohn, Anthony E. Zuiker

Season 4
4.1 *Assume Nothing*
(tx 25 September 2003)
dir. Richard J. Lewis, wr. Anthony E. Zuiker, Danny Cannon
4.2 *All for Our Country*
(tx 2 October 2003)
dir. Richard J. Lewis, tele. Andrew Lipsitz, Carol Mendelsohn, st. Richard Catalani
4.3 *Homebodies*
(tx 9 October 2003)
dir. Kenneth Fink, wr. Naren Shankar, Sarah Goldfinger
4.4 *Feeling the Heat*
(tx 23 October 2003)
dir. Kenneth Fink, wr. Anthony E. Zuiker, Eli Talbert

4.5 *Fur and Loathing*
(tx 30 October 2003)
dir. Richard J. Lewis, wr. Jerry Stahl
4.6 *Jackpot*
(tx 6 November 2003)
dir. Danny Cannon, wr. Naren Shankar, Carol Mendelsohn
4.7 *Invisible Evidence*
(tx 13 November 2003)
dir. Danny Cannon, wr. Josh Berman
4.8 *After the Show*
(tx 20 November 2003)
dir. Kenneth Fink, wr. Andrew Lipsitz, Elizabeth Devine
4.9 *Grissom Versus the Volcano*
(tx 11 December 2003)
dir. Richard J. Lewis, tele. Anthony E. Zuiker, Carol Mendelsohn, st. Josh Berman
4.10 *Coming of Rage*
(tx 18 December 2003)
dir. Nelson McCormick, tele. Sarah Goldfinger, st. Richard Catalani
4.11 *Eleven Angry Jurors*
(tx 8 January 2004)
dir. Matt Earl Beesley, wr. Josh Berman, Andrew Lipsitz
4.12 *Butterflied*
(tx 15 January 2004)
dir. Richard J. Lewis, wr. David Rambo
4.13 *Suckers*
(tx 5 February 2004)
dir. Danny Cannon, wr. Danny Cannon, Josh Berman
4.14 *Paper or Plastic?*
(tx 12 February 2004)
dir. Kenneth Fink, wr. Naren Shankar
4.15 *Early Rollout*
(tx 19 February 2004)
dir. Duane Clark, tele. Anthony E. Zuiker, Carol Mendelsohn, st. Elizabeth Devine
4.16 *Getting Off*
(tx 26 February 2004)
dir. Kenneth Fink, wr. Jerry Stahl
4.17 *XX*
(tx 4 March 2004)
dir. Deran Sarafian, wr. Ethlie Ann Vare

4.18 *Bad to the Bone*
(tx 1 April 2004)
dir. David Grossman, wr. Eli Talbert
4.19 *Bad Words*
(tx 15 April 2004)
dir. Rob Bailey, wr. Sarah Goldfinger
4.20 *Dead Ringer*
(tx 29 April 2004)
dir. Kenneth Fink, wr. Elizabeth Devine
4.21 *Turning of the Screw*
(tx 6 May 2004)
dir. Deran Sarafian, tele. Josh Berman, st. Carol Mendelsohn, Richard Catalani
4.22 *No More Bets*
(tx 13 May 2004)
dir. Richard J. Lewis, tele. Naren Shankar, Carol Mendelsohn, Judy McCreary, st. Dustin Lee Abraham, Andrew Lipsitz
4.23 *Bloodlines*
(tx 20 May 2004)
dir. Kenneth Fink, tele. Carol Mendelsohn, Naren Shankar, st. Eli Talbert, Sarah Goldfinger

Season 5
5.1 *Viva Las Vegas*
(tx 23 September 2004)
dir. Danny Cannon, wr. Danny Cannon, Carol Mendelsohn
5.2 *Down the Drain*
(tx 7 October 2004)
dir. Kenneth Fink, wr. Naren Shankar
5.3 *Harvest*
(tx 14 October 2004)
dir. David Grossman, wr. Judy McCreary
5.4 *Crow's Feet*
(tx 21 October 2004)
dir. Richard J. Lewis, wr. Josh Berman
5.5 *Swap Meet*
(tx 28 October 2004)
dir. Danny Cannon, wr. Carol Mendelsohn, David Rambo, Naren Shankar

151

153

8.2 *A La Cart*
(tx 4 October 2007)
dir. Richard J. Lewis,
wr. Richard Catalani, Sarah
Goldfinger
8.3 *Go to Hell*
(tx 11 October 2007)
dir. Jeffrey Hunt, wr. Douglas
Petrie
8.4 *The Case of the Cross-
Dressing Carp*
(tx 18 October 2007)
dir. Alec Smight,
wr. Jacqueline Hoyt, David
Rambo
8.5 *The Chick Chop Flick
Shop*
(tx 1 November 2007)
dir. Richard J. Lewis, wr. Evan
Dunsky
8.6 *Who and What*
(tx 8 November 2007)
dir. Kenneth Fink, tele. Danny
Cannon, Richard Catalani,
st. Carol Mendelsohn, Naren
Shankar
8.7 *Goodbye and Good Luck*
(tx 15 November 2007)
dir. Kenneth Fink, tele. Allen
MacDonald, Naren Shankar,
st. Sarah Goldfinger, Allen
MacDonald
8.8 *You Kill Me*
(tx 22 November 2007)
dir. Paris Barclay, tele. Douglas
Petrie, Naren Shankar,
st. Naren Shankar, Sarah
Goldfinger
8.9 *Cockroaches*
(tx 6 December 2007)
dir. William Friedkin,
wr. Dustin Lee Abraham
8.10 *Lying Down with Dogs*
(tx 13 December 2007)
dir. Michael Slovis, wr. Michael
F. X. Daley, Christopher
Barbour
8.11 *Bull*
(tx 10 January 2008)
dir. Richard J. Lewis,
tele. David Rambo, st. David
Rambo, Steven Felder

8.12 *Grissom's Divine Comedy*
(tx 3 April 2008)
dir. Richard J. Lewis,
tele. Jacqueline Hoyt,
st. Jacqueline Hoyt, Carol
Mendelsohn
8.13 *A Thousand Days on Earth*
(tx 10 April 2008)
dir. Kenneth Fink, wr. Evan
Dunsky
8.14 *Drop's Out*
(tx 24 April 2008)
dir. Jeffrey Hunt, tele. Dustin
Lee Abraham, Allen
MacDonald, st. Dustin Lee
Abraham, Naren Shankar
8.15 *The Theory of Everything*
(tx 1 May 2008)
dir. Christopher Leitch,
tele. Douglas Petrie, David
Rambo, st. Carol Mendelsohn,
David Rambo
8.16 *Two and a Half Deaths*
(tx 8 May 2008)
dir. Alec Smight, wr. Lee
Aronsohn, Chuck Lorre
8.17 *For Gedda*
(tx 15 May 2008)
dir. Kenneth Fink, tele. Dustin
Lee Abraham, Richard
Catalani, st. Dustin Lee
Abraham, Kenneth Fink

**Crime Scene Investigation
[pilot]**

USA/2000

directed by
Danny Cannon
producers
Cynthia Chvatal
William Petersen
written by
Anthony E. Zuiker
created by
Anthony E. Zuiker
director of photography
Gale Tattersall
edited by
Alex Mackie
Alec Smight
production designer
Richard J. Holland
composer
John M. Keane

© CBS Worldwide Inc. and
Alliance Atlantis Productions,
Inc.
Production Companies
Jerry Bruckheimer Films
Alliance Atlantis
CBS Productions

executive producers
Carol Mendelsohn
Ann Donahue
Jerry Bruckheimer
co-executive producers
James C. Hart
Anthony E. Zuiker
consulting producer
Jonathan Littman
associate producer
Philip Conserva
unit production manager
Chip Vucelich
production co-ordinator
Jean Costello
location manager
Ron Carr
post-production co-ordinator
Nancy Van Doornewaard
assistant directors
1st: Nilo Otero
2nd: Allen Kupetsky
2nd 2nd: Stacy Murphy
script supervisor
Susan Youngman
casting by
April Webster
Elizabeth Greenberg
camera operator
Ted Chu
gaffer
Jim Dillinger
key grip
Lloyd Barcroft
visual effects supervisor
Larry Detwiler
digital effects by
Infinity Digital Imaging, Inc.
assistant editors
Sandy Solowitz
Erik Presant
set decorator
Brenda Meyers-Ballard
property master
Tom Cahill
construction co-ordinator
Mark LaPresle

costume designer
Dan Lester
costume supervisor
Katina Kerr
key make-up artist
Perro Sorel
special effects make-up
Tom Burman
Barry Burman
hairstylist
Trish Almeida
music editor
Stan Jones
soundtrack
'Who Are You' by Pete
Townshend, performed by The
Who
production sound mixer
Will Yarbrough
re-recording mixers
Ross Davis
Larry Benjamin
Grover Helmsly
supervising sound editor
Mace Matiosian
sound effects editor
David Van Slyke
stunt co-ordinator
Jeff Cadiente
transportation co-ordinator
Don Tardino

high-definition post-production
by
Encore
promotional consideration
furnished by
Kodak

cast
William Petersen
Gil Grissom
Marg Helgenberger
Catherine Willows
Gary Dourdan
Warrick Brown
George Eads
Nick Stokes
Paul Guilfoyle
Captain Jim Brass
John Pyper-Ferguson
husband
Harrison Young
Judge Cohen
Allan Rich
Dr Gary Klausbach
Susan Gibney
Charlotte Meridian
Eric Szmanda
Greg Sanders
Royce D. Applegate
Mr Laferty
Barbara Tarbuck
Paige Harmon

Nancy Fish
liquor store owner
Cedrick Terrell
Boe Wilson
Chandra West
Holly Gribbs
Skip O'Brien
Sergeant Ray O'Riley
Matt O'Toole
Paul Millander
Greg Collins
Officer Arvington
Aasif Mandvi
Dr Leever
John Henry Whitaker
Jimmy
Madison McReynolds
Lindsey Willows
Garland Whitt
black male
Ashley [Ashly] Holloway
Laura Scott
Jeff Snyder
Officer Smith
Jane Leigh Connelly
wife
Joseph Patrick Kelly
hotel security
Terra Gold
Gina Harmon

155

Index

Page numbers in *italics* indicate illustrations.
n = endnote.

Also Published:

Buffy the Vampire Slayer
Anne Billson
Doctor Who
Kim Newman
Edge of Darkness
John Caughie
The League of Gentlemen
Leon Hunt
The Likely Lads
Phil Wickham
The Office
Ben Walters

Our Friends in the North
Michael Eaton
Queer as Folk
Glyn Davis
Seinfeld
Nicholas Mirzoeff
Seven Up
Stella Bruzzi
The Singing Detective
Glen Creeber
Star Trek
Ina Rae Hark